JOSHUA JAY'S BOOK OF
AMAZING
CARD
TRICKS

WORKMAN PUBLISHING · NEW YORK

Library of Congress Cataloging-in-Publication Data is available.

ISBN 978-0-7611-7822-4

Originally published as *Joshua Jay's Amazing Book of Cards*, now revised and abridged.

Workman books are available at special discounts when purchased in bulk for premiums and sales promotions as well as for fund-raising or educational use. Special editions or book excerpts can also be created to specification. For details, contact the Special Sales Director at the address below or send an email to specialmarkets@workman.com.

Interior design by Julie Duquet

Workman Publishing Company, Inc.
225 Varick Street
New York, NY 10014-4381
workman.com

WORKMAN is a registered trademark of Workman Publishing Co., Inc.

Printed in China
First printing May 2010

10 9 8 7 6 5 4 3

Photography credits

Cover photograph composite: Evan Sklar.
Original photography by David Arky: iii, 8, 9, 10, 11, 12 (top), 13, 14 (all on left), 15, 16 (top left & top right), 17, 18, 19, 20, 21 (all on left), 22, 23 (top & middle), 24, 25 (top left & top right), 26, 27 (top left & bottom left), 28, 29, 32, 33, 34, 35 (top), 36, 37, 38, 39 (all on left), 40 (bottom), 41, 42, 43, 44, 45, 46, 47, 48, 49, 50, 51 (top left, top right, bottom left), 54, 55, 56 (top left & top right), 57, 58, 59, 60, 61, 62 (top left & bottom left), 63, 64, 65, 66, 67, 70, 71 (top left & top right), 72, 73, 74, 75, 78, 79, 80 (top left & bottom left), 82, 83, 84, 85, 86, 87, 88, 89, 90, 91.

Original photography by Joshua Jay and Eric Ryan Anderson: 3, 4, 6, 23 (bottom), 30, 35 (bottom), 51 (bottom right), 52, 62 (right), 68, 69, 71 (bottom), 76, 92, 93, 94, 100.

Original photography by Evan Sklar: 56 (bottom).

Courtesy of Cláudio Décourt p. 14 (bottom), p. 25 (bottom row), p. 49 (top); Dover Publications, Inc. p. 1, p. 7, p. 49 (bottom row), p. 53, p. 77, p. 95; From the collection of Steve Forte p. 16 (bottom row); Chris Mattison/Getty Images p. 12 (bottom); Courtesy of The International Brotherhood of Magicians p. 89 (top left); Courtesy of Joshua Jay p. 81; Courtesy of Ralk Laue p. 21 (right); Melissa Lucier p. i; Mary Evans Picture Library p. 27 (right); Courtesy of The Society for American Magicians p. 96 (bottom left); Sophia Su p. 39 (right).

CONTENTS

At the ripe age of 5, my mother gave me a strange gift. It was a deck of cards that her mother gave her. It immediately became my most prized possession and I never went anywhere without it. One day, a sweet librarian at the local Brooklyn library sat me down with a book of simple self-working card magic. Little did I know this would change my world forever. With just a deck of cards I had the ability to amaze anyone.

Joshua Jay was also introduced to playing cards at a young age. Since then, he has traveled the globe, cards in hand, and along the way has uncovered a wealth of information: shuffles, arcane playing card history, hilarious scams, and, of course, some amazing magic effects. I consider Josh an important emerging voice in our art. He is an incredible author, and I'm pleased that he has succeeded here—with this extraordinary celebration of cards, an easy-to-follow guide that will teach you some truly remarkable feats.

— DAVID BLAINE
New York City

Introduction

Cards are power. Learn how to harness that power, and you'll be forever rewarded.

—JAMES SWAIN, *21st Century Card Magic*

Playing cards is addictive. So are the playing cards themselves. My habit has me up to two packs a day. Next time you're in a bookstore, check out the gaming section. You'll notice several shelves packed tight with titles on card games, strategies, and "winning" formulas—all with outlandish claims of possessing the ultimate get-rich equation.

Now look down a shelf and to your right—after the crossword puzzles but before the role-playing games. You're in the section on magic tricks—a subject and art form I have studied and practiced continually since I was eight years old.

Between books about card games and magic manuals, there's an abyss. I've attempted to fill that void here. This book picks up after the card games stop and before the real magic tricks begin.

In the pages that follow, you'll learn card games you *can't* lose, exotic ways to shuffle, astounding card miracles, sleight of hand, high-speed card throwing, how to memorize a deck in less than 10 seconds, and much more. You'll use them at work, at play, on your desk, and in the bar (after page 32, you'll never have to buy a drink again). But gambling isn't the only way to get hooked on cards. With a manageable amount of practice, you can become the local card whiz, whipping out fans and flourishes quicker than a gunslinger on the draw.

Some of the material in this book requires lots of practice to really make it look smooth. Other tricks can be done instantly, while you're reading. In all cases, I break down each technique into manageable, easy-to-learn actions, with photographs at every step.

I've got three suggestions for you as you carve your path to card awesomeness. First, learn the contents of this book in the order they appear. You can jump around if you want—I won't be offended. But the shuffling skills you learn in Chapter 1 will serve you well when you want to cheat at cards in Chapter 4 or dazzle your friends with tricks in Chapter 2. I've also rated the level of difficulty of each item, so you know what you're getting into. Stunts are rated 1 through 4 (represented visually by the four suits ♠♣♦♥), with level 1 being the most approachable—these are tricks or flourishes you can work instantly. A stunt rated 2 or 3 requires some practice. And a 4 might be more of an investment—it could take you three weeks of daily practice or longer to master. Seconds, minutes, hours, days—all spent with a deck of cards. Sounds like bliss to me.

Second, note the materials list—often you don't need more than the pack of cards included here but sometimes a crisp, new deck is warranted, whereas other times that old, soft-edged deck will do. In some instances, a new deck will make an effect infinitely easier to perform.

Third, put this book down, pick up the pack of cards, and watch the accompanying 106-minute DVD we've included in the kit. The DVD features performances and tutorials for the 29 tricks and stunts found in the book—plus two bonus effects that you won't find in these pages! I demonstrate some of my favorite magic effects, flashy flourishes, and bizarre shuffles, each one at performance speed; and then I teach the techniques. Use the DVD in conjunction with the book—read and cue up your disc to follow along with the tutorial—*or,* watch the DVD first, to inspire the basic moves, and then polish your techniques with the extra detail provided in the following pages.

Soon, a deck of cards will no longer be a way to pass the time; it might well become your way of life. Just grab the deck and keep reading.

LET'S GET STARTED

A pack of cards has long been shrouded in mystery and deception. You're about to learn its secrets and how to dazzle people using just these 52 pieces of pasteboard (and maybe a couple jokers). Let's start with the first three lessons. Just answer this question first and then turn to page 4: How many of these nine cards are red?

Continued

❧ WELCOME BACK ❧

continued from page 3

There are five red cards, of course. I have no doubt you guessed that. But this question is misdirection, to conceal three other deceptions noted with callouts in the otherwise identical photo below:

Note that I asked you how many of the nine cards are red—but did you count the total or did you take my word for it? There are actually ten cards. Always make your opponents show you their hand. Always check twice. Always count. And always cut the cards.

And I'm sure you noticed that I'm holding the cards so you can see them. But did you notice that I was sporting an extra finger? That's sleight of hand, but with a fifth finger, it's most certainly not slight of hand. If you're trying to bust a cheat or solve a magic trick, heed this lesson: Cards only come to life when held between deft fingers. Pay closer attention to the hands than the cards.

Most surprising, I'll bet you didn't notice that the Ten of Hearts . . . is black! Even though the secret is right in front of our eyes, we don't see it because we aren't expecting it. Make no assumptions about playing cards.

There are 10 cards shown, not 9.

The Ten of Hearts is red!

Where did the extra finger come from?

Playing Card Basics

Trying to learn the card stunts that follow without understanding the lingo would be like stepping into a hockey rink for a game without knowing how to skate (although here your teeth are not in jeopardy—not until the second chapter). Acquaint yourself with this basic terminology and form before proceeding:

Dealers' Grip. Hold the cards in your left hand, as if you were dealing cards for a game. The thumb rests along the left side, the index finger curls around the front of the deck, and the other finger pads rest on the right side.

NOTE: For ease of explanation, the stunts in this book are described for right-handed folks. If you're left-handed, simply reverse the actions.

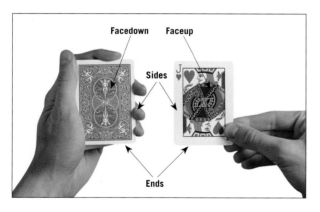

The Parts of a Pasteboard. Pasteboard is another term for playing cards, derived from a time when the front of a card was "pasted" onto its back. Here are some basic terms to know when handling a pack of pasteboards (otherwise known as a deck of cards).

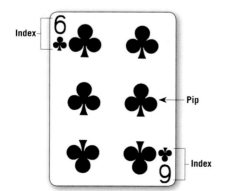

Index and Pip. Several of the stunts described in this book require precise finger placement. The index portion is the part of the card with numbers or letters in the corner. Some European cards have four indices (one in each corner), but cards in the United States generally only have an index in the upper left and lower right. A pip is a suit symbol: A Six of Clubs has six Club "pips" (or eight, actually, if you count the two small symbols paired with the index).

Chapter 1

All Hands on Deck

. . . in shewing feats, and juggling with cards,
the principall point consisteth in shuffling them nimblie.

—Reginald Scot, *Discoverie of Witchcraft*, 1584

Reginald Scot, arguably the first English author to discuss uses for playing cards other than traditional card games, knew well the importance of handling a deck "nimblie."

Today we call this a "card flourish"—which is magicians' jargon for showing off. Magicians use flourishes to demonstrate dexterity. Most card flourishes look incredibly difficult because, well, they are. That being said, there are also a few smooth-as-silk moves that look master-level difficult but are in fact easy to learn and execute. Imagine the fear on your poker opponents' faces when they pull up their chairs around the table and see you fanning the deck with one hand, flipping the deck from one hand to the other, and casually cutting the cards one-handed.

The Ribbon Spread and Flip

MATERIALS: A new deck of playing cards, a soft but firm surface   LEVEL: ♠ ♣ ♦ ♥

This flourish will wow any audience. Cards cascade from one side of the table to the other without you touching them! It's ideally performed on a firm but soft surface such as a tablecloth, carpeting, or a padded card table. Stay away from glass, Formica, or tiled tabletops, which cause the edges of the cards to slip.

1. Place the deck facedown on the left side of your work surface. Place your right hand on top of the tabled deck, gripping the pack by the ends between the thumb and fingers. Slide your first finger so it's positioned along the left side of the pack.

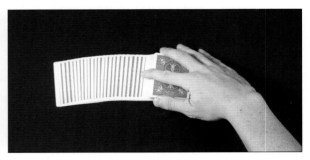

2. In one smooth action, smear the cards from left to right in a 20-inch spread, pressing gently along the side of the pack with your first finger to ensure the cards are distributed evenly. A quick, firm motion will encourage equal spacing between the cards (breaking tempo will cause the cards to clump and cluster). Practice the spread a dozen times before moving on to the next step; it's important your spread is even and straight.

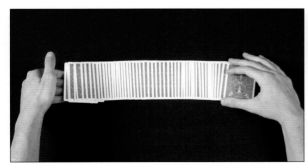

3. Position your left hand at the left side of the spread as you move your right hand to the right end of the spread. Maneuver the pads of the left fingers under the leftmost bottom card. (Alternatively, begin with your left fingers in this position in Step 1.)

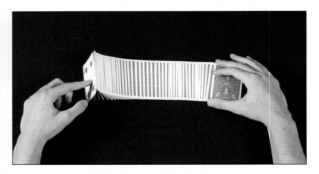

4. With the left fingers, carefully lift the left edge of the card, pivoting it up and to the right. Take care to leave the card's right side on the table.

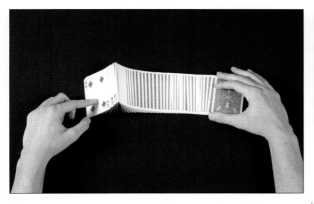

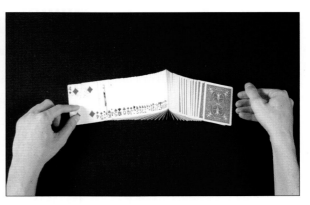

5. Swiftly push down on the leftmost card, causing the card to flip faceup.

6. In a chain reaction, the rest of the deck will also flip faceup, domino-style.

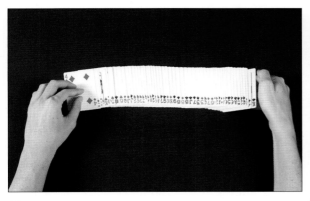

7. The slickest part of this flourish is that the right end of the deck flips faceup directly into the awaiting right fingers.

8. Now scoop the deck by sweeping with your right hand toward the left.

One-Handed Flip

MATERIALS: A new deck of playing cards, a soft but firm surface   **LEVEL: ♠ ♣ ◆ ♥**

At this point, you probably think there's nothing more entertaining in the entire world than two-handed ribbon-spread flips (the Ribbon Spread and Flip, page 8). Wrong. Because you're about to do the same thing—but with one hand tied behind your back. I know, it's going to be mind-blowing.

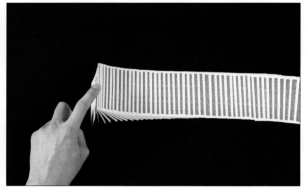

1. Follow Steps 1 through 3 in the Ribbon Spread and Flip, page 8, sliding the first finger of your left hand under the leftmost card.

2. Slowly glide your finger across the edges of the cards in the ribbon spread, allowing your finger to fluidly "ride" the cards like a surfer rides a wave.

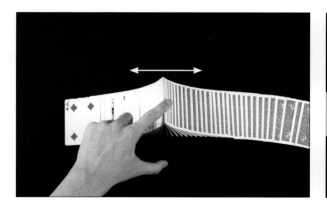

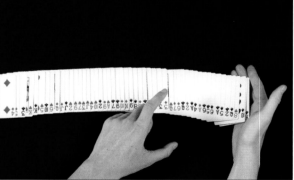

3. Practice maintaining this position while moving your finger back and forth along the length of the spread.

4. To finish the flourish, position your right hand to the right of the spread's center and release your grip from the cards. They will cascade domino-style, to the right side of the spread.

No-Handed Flip

MATERIALS: A new deck of playing cards, a soft but firm surface   LEVEL: ♠ ♣ ♦ ♥

In this variation, you cascade the deck of cards back and forth with ease. The tension of the deck is balanced on the edge of a single separate card. This action is referred to as "Walking the Dog."

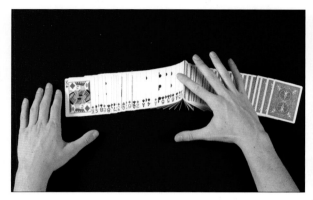

1. Follow Steps 1 through 3 in the Ribbon Spread and Flip, page 8, to begin with an evenly distributed ribbon spread. Initiate the flip at the leftmost point of the spread and allow the cards to glide along your right fingertip.

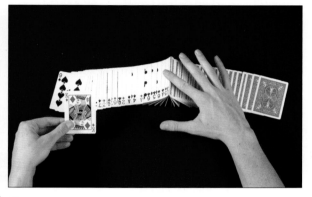

2. Since you are in the midst of the flip, the left side of the deck is faceup. With your left hand, pick up the leftmost card between your left thumb and fingers.

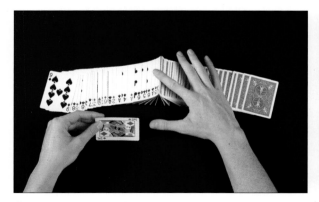

3. To transfer control of the ribbon spread from your right finger to the playing card in your left hand, hold the card in your left hand, perpendicular to the floor, so that you can see its face.

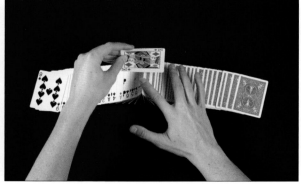

4. Balance the bottom edge of the card crosswise on the apex of the ribbon spread.

Continued

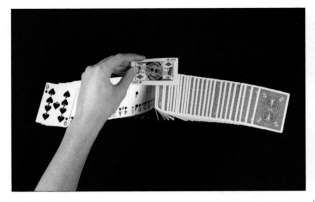

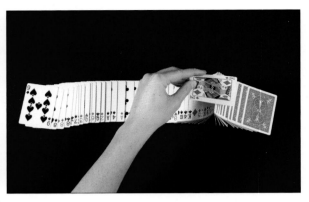

5. Slowly remove your finger, leaving the card edge in contact with the spread. The wave remains!

6. Move the left hand to the right and back to the left, all the while controlling the apex of the spread . . . without touching it directly.

SLITHERING SNAKES AND SLICK SPREADS

David Hu, a Georgia Tech–based mechanical engineer and researcher, has made some groundbreaking discoveries about the way snakes move. And to communicate his findings, he compares a slithering snake to a ribbon spread deck of cards, just like the one described here.

Scientists previously attributed snake locomotion to pushing against obstacles like shrubs, plants, or rocks that lay in their paths. But Hu studied the motion of snakes on smooth surfaces, and came to a different conclusion. He discovered that the stomach scales on a snake overlap like "a spread of cards," which allows them to grip even a smooth surface to support the snake's body as it lifts itself up and forward. You can see precisely how this would work when you execute a ribbon spread: Examine how each overlapping card in the spread grips your working surface so it can bear the weight of the surrounding cards.

No-Handed Flip Plus

MATERIALS: A new deck of playing cards, a soft but firm surface   LEVEL: ♠♣♦♥

Ready to take it to the next level? The No-Handed Flip Plus begins where the No-Handed Flip left off. While this isn't the most difficult flourish in the book, it *looks* that way, and that's enough to intimidate your Texas Hold 'Em opponents. If you've already mastered the No-Handed Flip, skip to Step 4.

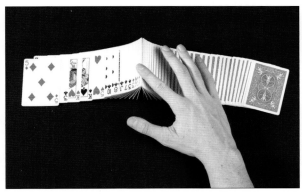

1. Begin in the starting position of a No-Handed Flip, page 11, with your right first fingertip gliding along the ribbon spread's apex.

2. Pick up the leftmost card between your left thumb and fingers.

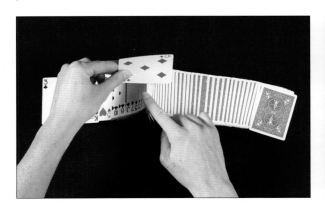

3. Transfer control of the ribbon spread from your right finger to the playing card in your left hand. Hold the card in your left hand, perpendicular to the floor.

4. While maintaining the spread's apex with the card in the left hand, grasp *another* card with your right hand, perhaps from the right end of the ribbon spread.

Continued 🖝

5. Mirroring the actions of the left hand, position the card in your right hand on the apex of the spread, in the same place as the card in your left hand.

6. Simultaneously, move your hands in opposite directions. The left hand glides its card to the left as the right hand glides its card to the right. With a delicate touch, it will look like the photo above.

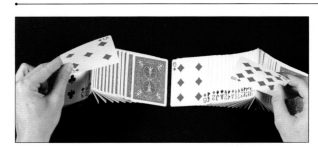

7. That is, you can *split* the apex, gliding half the spread to the left and the other half to the right. There. Now go practice your ribbon spreads.

CARD QUIZ

Is the Nine of Diamonds cursed?

Maybe. Since the 18th century, the Nine of Diamonds has carried the nickname "the Curse of Scotland." The reason for this nickname is still debated by playing card historians. The stories possess the same "yeah right" element, but I prefer the grimmest theory. In 1692, Sir John Dalrymple contributed significantly to the Massacre of Glencoe, in which 38 Highland clansmen were killed. Dalrymple's coat of arms had nine diamondlike lozenges that are similar to the design on the Nine of Diamonds. Some contend that the order for the massacre was signed on the back of an actual Nine of Diamonds.

Two-Handed Fan

MATERIALS: A new deck of playing cards   **LEVEL:** ♠ ♣ ♦ ♡

A fan of cards is iconic. No, a fanned deck won't keep you cool on a hot day at the beach, but this flourish may make you look a little bit cooler in that bathing suit.

The key to this flourish is the condition of the pack. Forget about trying to fan your grandma's solitaire cards—after even minimal use, residue from your working surface collects on the cards, rendering them useless for tasks such as fanning and ribbon spreading. Brand-new cards, however, spread like butter.

1. Begin with the pack faceup, gripped from above in the right hand and from beneath in the left hand.

2. Place the inner left corner of the pack onto the webbing of the left thumb. You'll also note that the deck is situated in the left palm at an angle. This positioning will give the fan its symmetry later.

3. Extend your right first finger and place it on the left side of the pack, just below the outer left corner. The tip of the first finger should be at the same level as the lowermost card of the deck. The left thumb clamps down on the uppermost card of the pack.

Continued 👉

4. The first finger facilitates the fanning action. You'll move the finger in a clockwise, circular motion around the left hand, smearing the cards as you go. At the same time, the left first finger must move up slightly as it rotates, allowing its tip to graze every card during the action. The cards pivot under the left thumb, which remains in a clamped position.

5. If you end up with a large block of cards in an unspread condition on top of the pack, then you need to lift your left first finger more as you're fanning. Also, keep in mind that the left fingers play no part in the fanning action and remain stationary beneath the pack throughout. The cards in your fan should be evenly distributed, which is a result of a fast spreading action.

CARD QUIZ

Did each card always have an index in the corners?

Actually, no. Before 1864, playing cards were only distinguishable by the suit pips across the face of the card. This required a card player to view every card completely to discern its value. Spreading cards this much made glimpsing an opponent's hand too easy.

An early solution to the problem, called "Triplicates," used a small picture of the entire card in the corners. Now a rare collector's item, Triplicate cards could be fanned tightly while allowing a player to see his entire hand of cards. Now, when you fan a deck of cards or hold a dealt hand between your fingers, you can easily see the values of all the cards, thanks to the indexes on each corner.

Blank Fan

MATERIALS: **A deck of playing cards**   LEVEL: ♠ ♣ ♦ ♥

What do you do with a blank deck? Well, you can use it in an easy but impressive flourish that is especially effective with a borrowed deck, say before a game of cards—you can make any deck look like a trick deck. The identifying indices on playing cards are printed on the upper-left and lower-right corners (see diagram on page 5), which makes a traditional left-handed fan appear quite flashy. However, if you carry out the mechanics of a Two-Handed Fan with the deck in your right hand, not a single index is displayed except the one on the face of the deck.

1. Begin by cutting the Ace of Diamonds to the face of the deck. This card has the smallest area of ink on it, which makes it easy to disguise as a card without anything printed on it.

2. With the cards held in the *right* hand, execute a tight Two-Handed Fan (see page 15 for reference). No color should be visible. If any part of a card's suit is exposed, make tiny adjustments to the cards with the left fingers.

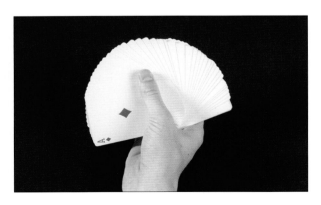

3. Place the right thumb pad on top of the Ace's outer right index, covering it from view.

Continued 👉

4. With the left thumb, cover the Diamond pip in the center of the card plus the inner right Ace index. You're holding the fan with two hands, which allows you to conceal the Ace of Diamonds. The result is a completely whitewashed pack!

BLANK BACKS: A FAILED EXPERIMENT

It was a logical solution, so I can't blame them. Nineteenth-century card gaming was rife with cheating (on Mississippi riverboats, in tent-towns, at saloon games, and so on). Cards were marked (modified) by cheaters, and many card back designs were copied and printed with markings.

To combat these nefarious practices, card manufacturers instituted a bold solution: There would be no printing on card backs at all. The theory was that if there was no artwork to modify, any attempted marking would be obvious.

But cheats are as resourceful as they are greedy. Even though the backs appeared as blank (as in the Blank Fan taught here), cheats began marking the cards with dirt smudges. These tiny blemishes appeared to be nothing more than normal wear and tear, but to the informed cheat, the smudge was an easily identifiable mark. Cheats also developed a system for marking the *side* of each card. Called edgework, an unscrupulous player could nick the edge of all the high cards during play, and then sight these markings during subsequent rounds.

Giant Fan

MATERIALS: **A deck of playing cards**   LEVEL: ♠♣♦ ♥

If you're of the opinion that bigger is always better, then try this double-decker fan. It's an easy flourish to execute and the perfect way to impress your friends (and your enemies, too!) the next time you sit down at the card table.

1. Begin with the deck faceup as if you are about to deal cards in left dealing position.

2. With your left thumb, push the top card into the right hand.

3. Move the left hand forward and push the end of the second card until it protrudes halfway from the deck. In magic terminology, this is called "outjogging" a card.

4. Retract the left hand so it is once again even with the right, and push the third card over to the right hand. Outjog the fourth card and repeat this process with the rest of the deck. *Note:* Outjogging is admittedly tedious, and you can achieve the same results in seconds once you've mastered the Faro Shuffle (see page 65).

Continued 👉

5. When you've exhausted every card, gently square the sides of the elongated deck. The two packets should be interlaced (overlapped) about 1 inch.

6. Hold the packet that is closest to the body (the inner packet) in dealing grip, allowing the outer packet to protrude from the left hand.

7. Then spread the cards in a gentle arc between your left thumb and fingers . . .

8. . . . bracing the back of the fan from beneath with your right hand.

Variation: For a more challenging move in Step 7, smear the right first finger in a clockwise motion.

Allow the left hand's cards to spread evenly, carrying out the same mechanics as a Two-Handed Fan (page 15).

Brace the spread at the area where the cards from both packets overlap.

CARD QUIZ

How big is the largest card fan?

The largest card fan included 326 cards, a world record held by Ralf Laue. On March 18, 1994, he held those 326 cards in a one-handed fan so that every index was visible.

One-Handed Fan

MATERIALS: A new deck of playing cards   LEVEL: ♠ ♣ ♦ ♥

Mastering a sleight or flourish and then learning to do it with one hand is a recurring theme in this book, but keep these points in mind: First, flourishes with one hand look more impressive than two-handed stunts because they appear more difficult. Second, they often are more difficult—this item included. Third, think of all the cool things you can do with your other, free hand. You could scramble some eggs, play fetch with your dog, or hand out high fives!

The One-Handed Fan actually bears little resemblance to the Two-Handed Fan. The hand position is different, and the fanning action, this time performed with the left fingers, actually moves in a counterclockwise direction.

1. The key to the One-Handed Fan lies in the starting position, so be precise with your grip. With your left hand, grip the pack (faceup) at the very end with the left thumb pad pressing against the uppermost card and running parallel along its end.

2. The left finger pads contact the lowermost card. Curl the left fingers and, like the left thumb, grip the pack at its very end.

3. Holding the left thumb relatively still, slowly straighten and extend the left fingers, causing the cards to spread and fan in a counterclockwise rotation.

4. As the fingers extend, the left thumb moves only slightly to the right, allowing the uppermost batch of cards to fan. The hardest part is getting the cards to curve around the hand. At first you'll find your One-Handed Fans almost linear in shape, but as you become more limber at uncurling your left fingers, the fans will gradually become more circular. Practice to develop a feel for the pressure you need to apply between your thumb and fingers: Your grip has to be firm enough to keep the cards held in a fanned position but loose enough to allow each card to spread.

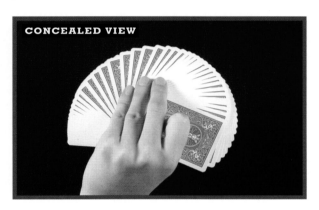

CONCEALED VIEW

Variation: As with the Two-Handed Fan (page 15), if you learn to fan the cards with your right hand, you'll have the added bonus of showing the deck blank (see Blank Fan, page 17).

THE CARD SHOE BLUES

The card shoe is a gaming device, a version of which was devised by John Scarne, to prevent corrupt dealers from false dealing. But even the shoes themselves can be gaffed. The shoe depicted here is a rare "Two Shoe," named so because it can be used to deal the *second* card from the top. It also has a reflective, embedded prism near the top that divulges the identity of the top facedown, giving the dealer another unfair advantage.

One-Handed Cut

MATERIALS: A deck of playing cards **LEVEL:** ♠ ♣ ♦ ♡

"**C**ut 'em," your hotshot poker opponent says as he drops the deck on the table. Who is this guy, and why is he using that tone with you? No biggie. You pick up the cards, yawn, and cut them with one hand. He swallows hard. This is called intimidation. For best results, you have to *play down* these flourishes; they should look effortless.

Actually, the cut is called the Charlier (Shar-lee-ay) cut and was invented more than a hundred years ago by a French guy named . . . Charlier (just one name—think Madonna or Sting).

1. You'll need only one hand for this cut, so put your nondominant hand somewhere out of the way. Begin by holding the cards facedown in your dominant hand, using your thumb pad to support one side of the pack and your finger pads to grip the opposite side. Grip the deck at the very tips of the fingers, allowing for maximum space beneath the cards and your palm.

2. Bend your thumb slightly, easing your grip on the sides of the cards. Allow approximately half of the cards in the deck to drop down from the thumb onto the palm like it's hinged.

3. Curl your first finger and move it below the dropped packet.

4. Push up on the underside of the packet with the first finger.

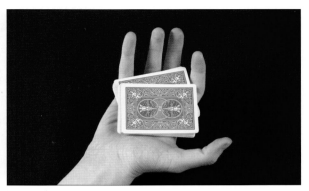

5. When the lower half of the deck clears the upper packet, let the upper packet fall . . .

6. . . . followed in quick succession by the second. (Release the thumb's grip on the cards, and both packets will collapse into your palm.)

CARD QUIZ

Where do playing cards come from?

Playing cards are thought to have originated in central Asia during the 10th century. They looked like flattened dominoes and were used for game play.

Playing cards spread through Persia to Egypt. In Egypt, the Mamluk people developed four suits for their cards: swords, polo sticks, cups, and coins, which represented aspects of daily life for Mamluk aristocracy. Four-suited cards reached the European gentry around 1370. These hand-painted cards were used for game play as well, but reserved mostly for royalty. Soldiers carried playing cards across the warpaths of Europe to England and France.

The French gave playing cards an overhaul, dressing the figures in 15th-century royal garb, and categorizing the cards into the four suits we use today: *Pique* (Spade), *Carreau* (Diamond), *Trèfle* (Club), and *Coeur* (Heart).

Five colorful court cards from 16th-century Rouen, France, illustrate the original royal dress.

Self-Cutting Deck

MATERIALS: A deck of playing cards, a bed or a chair   LEVEL: ♠ ♣ ♦ ♡

You could classify this as both a trick and a flourish. Either way, it's cool to see it work. But follow these instructions carefully, or you'll find yourself playing 52-card pickup. Here's the effect: Holding a deck of cards, extend your hand and ask someone to cut the cards. Just before his hand reaches the pasteboards, half the cards fly out of your left hand and into your awaiting right fingers—the deck cuts itself!

1. Hold the deck facedown, gripped between the thumb and finger pads of your left hand, in an elevated position. Curl the left first finger around the front end of the pack. *Tip:* Sit to practice this effect (it's far easier to gather cards from your lap than from the floor).

2. Extend your hand toward the card opponent or participant nearest you and ask him to cut the cards. Inconspicuously move the right hand between the left hand and your body in preparation for catching the lower half of the deck.

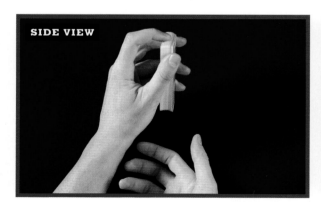

3. With your left first finger, gently contact the outer end of the pack.

4. Jerk your left first finger outward away from your body, projecting the lower portion of the deck into the palm of your right hand.

5. Catch the packet in the right hand and without pausing . . .

6. . . . place the packet on top of the cards in the left hand. This move is all attitude and timing. Think James Bond. The timing is like this: "Would you cut the cards?" Pause one beat, then execute the move. "Thanks, that's perfect."

CARD QUIZ

Where did the expression "not playing with a full deck" come from?

England, 1707. Queen Anne enforced a tax on playing cards that eventually affected both manufacturers and the public (this practice continued in the U.K. until 1960). In 1828, manufacturers placed the tax stamp on the Ace of Spades instead of the box. These stamps were taken seriously by the English government: One Richard Hardy was *executed* for forging such a stamped Ace. To avoid paying the inflated price, some English citizens began to purchase decks without any Aces of Spades. Hence they were "playing without a full deck."

Throwing Cards

MATERIALS: Several new playing cards   LEVEL: ♠♣♦♥

Thrown playing cards *can* be used for self-defense. Historically, scaling (another term for throwing) cards has almost always been reserved for a display of skill. Howard Thurston, America's foremost magician at the beginning of the nineteenth century, was known to scale hundreds of promotional cards into the audience at incredible speeds and distances—even into theater balconies.

Whether you're defending a damsel in distress or just have a desire to throw something fast enough to leave a mark, scaling a playing card is easier than it looks. Just make sure you aim away from innocent bystanders: Even playing cards can draw blood!

1. Begin by holding a playing card in your right hand. Rest the pad of your first finger on the edge of the outer left corner while you pinch the card between the thumb from above and the second finger from beneath.

What is the farthest distance a playing card has ever been thrown?

In the 1970s, expert sleight-of-hand artist Ricky Jay set world records for his card-throwing skills. Today, magician Rick Smith holds the world record. Smith used to be a pitcher at Cleveland State University, and perhaps it was this training that helped earn him the world's record: 216' 4" (at 92 miles per hour).

2. Curl your right hand in toward your body and flick the card forcefully, parallel with the ground, as you would throw a Frisbee.

3. The card must rotate off the first finger. If the card flutters to the ground just inches from your body, you either aren't getting enough rotation during the release or you're throwing the card at an angle (always aim to toss the card parallel with the ground).

4. Once you've got a working formula for throwing the card, practice increasing the force of your throw: Specifically, use more arm strength and focus on "snapping" the wrist as you release the card. Gym-goers, remember snapping towels in the locker room? Same move. When you scale a card properly, you'll know it. The card will whiz by at a speed disproportionate to the amount of force you applied.

Sleight of hand card magic has existed almost as long as cards themselves.

Chapter 2

Tricks

"Do you like card tricks?" he asked.

"No, I hate card tricks," I answered.

"Well, I'll just show you this one."

He showed me three.

—W. Somerset Maugham, *Mr. Know All*

"Do you like card tricks?" he asked.

I said no. He asked me if I liked knees to my groin. I said no.

He said, "Then take a card."

—Steve Beam, *Semi-Automatic Card Tricks, Volume 2*

Card magic is not only the ultimate party trick, it's an excellent way to bring friends together, entertain family, or break the ice with new people. Some card tricks take

a lifetime to perfect, but the effects in this chapter—all of professional caliber—can be mastered almost instantly.

As trick editor for *MAGIC* magazine, dozens of amazing card tricks appear in my mailbox every day. I've taken some of the best ideas from this publication and from the history of the art and made them

self-working. I've also given you a variety of effects, which will allow you to combine tricks and perform your own close-up show. This material is perfect for first dates, poker breaks, or wowing friends. A professional magician could earn a living with the card tricks described in this chapter. Try them as you read; you might even fool yourself.

The Card Shark

MATERIALS: A deck of playing cards   LEVEL: ♠ ♣ ♦ ♥

As if finding a spectator's card in the deck weren't enough, you also manage to produce a royal flush in Spades. *Warning:* Nobody will play cards with you after seeing this trick, so choose your marks wisely.

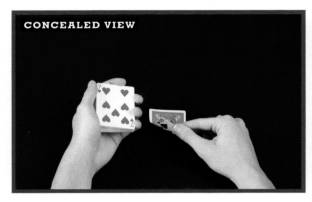

1. Pull the Ten of Spades from the deck and place it facedown on the table.

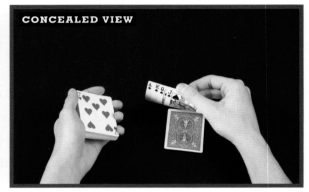

2. Place the Jack of Spades facedown on top, followed by the Queen, King, and Ace of Spades.

3. Next, place any Six, say the Six of Hearts, faceup on top of the pile. Place the rest of the deck facedown on top, and you're ready to begin. *Optional:* If you're feeling saucy, throw in a False Cut (see page 74).

4. Place the deck facedown on the table, saying, "I'll show you why you should never play cards with me."

5. Ask the participant to cut the cards, and place the cut-off packet on the table.

6. Ask her to remember the card she cut to, pointing to the card on top of the lower portion of the deck. Let's say this card is the Seven of Clubs.

7. Instruct her to place this card on top of the pile already in front of her (the original top half of the deck) . . .

8. . . . and complete the cut. While it appears that this process has hopelessly buried the participant's card, it has actually been positioned exactly six cards below the faceup Six.

Continued 👉

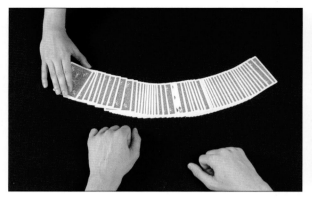

9. "I will now make your card appear faceup in the deck." Snap your fingers, shake your groove thing, or perform any gesture that could be construed as magic. Ask the participant to spread the deck facedown across the table. This will reveal the faceup Six of Hearts. To the spectator, this is unimpressive, as it appears your trick has failed.

10. Separate the deck at the faceup card, making the Six of Hearts the top card of the lower half of the spread. Square this portion of cards into a pile and hand it to the participant.

11. Feigning disappointment, ask, "You didn't pick the Six?" Appear to gather your thoughts. "I knew that. The Six is an indicator card; it's sending us a message. Why don't you count down six cards." Take the Six from the top of the participant's pile and display it. Instruct the participant to deal six cards onto your outstretched left hand.

12. As she deals the sixth card, ask her what card she selected (the Seven of Clubs). Instruct her to turn over the sixth card . . . the Seven of Clubs is revealed!

13. She's amazed. "But," you say, "that isn't the reason why you should never play cards with me. . . . " Draw attention to the five facedown cards she just dealt onto your hand. "*This* is why you should never play cards with me!" Dramatically reveal the contents of your hand: a royal flush in Spades.

CARD SHARPS AND CARD SHARKS

Card sharpers and card sharks both refer to nefarious gamblers. The term "sharper" (as in a player who is *sharper* than his opponents) first appeared in 1681, while the term "shark" was first used in a cheating context in 1599. Bottom line: For poker safety, avoid sharp objects and don't swim with sharks.

CARD QUIZ

How are playing cards made?

They're actually layered. Standard playing cards are composed of three layers made from fiber rags mixed with a china clay (the clay gives the pulp its white coloring). An adhesive made with carbon black is used to glue the pieces together; this adhesive adds to the opacity of each card. Casein and borax coatings are applied to the front and back, and this finish gives the cards their slick feel. Playing cards are printed on large sheets, which are then punched out for assembly and packaging.

One Ahead

MATERIALS: A deck of playing cards   LEVEL: ♠ ♣ ♦ ♥

This card trick, one of the oldest (and best) in the world, will come naturally to good poker players or great liars.

Oh, good, you're still here.

Magicians call this the one-ahead principle because you begin with prior knowledge of one of the three cards. In this way you can predict all three cards; but the *order* of the cards is a total bluff.

1. Ask someone to shuffle a deck thoroughly, and as they shuffle, secretly sight the top card of the deck. (*Note:* Sometimes this is easy; sometimes it's impossible.) Remember it. Let's assume it's the Three of Clubs.

If you can't see the top card during the participant's shuffle, glimpse the one on the bottom. This card is much easier to see.

2. Stress the fact that the participant has done all the shuffling and that you haven't touched the cards. Ask her to cut the deck into three piles.

3. Pay attention to where the glimpsed card (Three of Clubs) resides as the participant cuts. It will usually be on the left or the right, depending on whether you remembered the top or bottom card, and whether your participant cut right to left or left to right. It doesn't make any difference—you just have to secretly note where it is. Let's assume the Three of Clubs is on top of the rightmost pile.

4. "Despite your shuffling," you say, "I'm going to ascertain three cards by osmosis." So saying, place your first finger on the top card of the leftmost pile. (At this point you must always place your finger on a pile *other than* the one with the remembered card.) Close your eyes and concentrate, as if learning the identity of the card through your fingertips. Then proclaim, "This one is the Three of Clubs!"

5. Pick up that top card from this pile and hold it toward yourself in your left hand the way you would hold cards during a game. It's important that nobody else can see this card, and that you note the identity of this card. Let's say it's the King of Hearts. Even though this card is not the Three of Clubs (and you claimed it was), smile like you got it right.

Continued ☞

6. Place a finger on the other pile without the Three of Clubs (in our case this would be the middle pile). "This feels like the King of Hearts!" you say.

7. Pick up the card off the center pile and place it next to the card in your left hand. Casually notice its value; perhaps it's the Five of Spades. Again, act content with your guess.

8. Now put your finger on the last pile. Even though you know which card is on top (Three of Clubs), you must miscall this card. Call out the name of the card you just picked up from pile 2. "This last one I'm not sure about, but I'm pretty sure it's the Five of Spades."

9. Pick up the top card of the last pile with your right hand and transfer it *to the face of* the pair of cards in your left hand.

10. "I'll bet you don't believe me. See?" So saying, lower your hand so the participant can see the value of the cards.

11. Thumb over the top faceup card (the Three of Clubs) onto the left pile.

12. Then, in a continuing action, deal the King of Hearts onto the center pile, and finally drop the Five of Spades onto the last pile. Three cards by osmosis!

CARD QUIZ

Can cards tell time?

There are tall tales about cards that represent or are able to tell time, but there isn't any substantiating evidence to prove this. Still, the coincidences are staggering:

- Four seasons in a year and four suits in a deck.
- 13 lunar cycles of the moon and 13 cards in each suit.
- 52 weeks in a year and 52 cards in a deck. Also, if you count and add all the letters in the names of the 13 values (A-C-E is 3 plus T-W-O is 3 equals 6, and so on), the sum is exactly 52. (And, it even works in French.)
- 365 days in one year. If you add up the value of every card in the deck (11 for Jacks, 12 for Queens, 13 for Kings), the result is 364 . . . now add one for the Joker (the additional Joker is for use during leap years).

Pointer Power

MATERIALS: A deck of playing cards   LEVEL: ♠ ♣ ♦ ♥

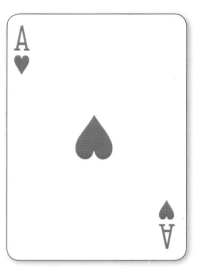

For obvious reasons, it doesn't seem that cards marked secretly on their *faces* would be of much use. But, you'll use an old magician's marking system on the face of certain playing cards to determine a chosen card.

Certain cards are known as "pointer" cards. By its design, the orientation on a pointer card is easily distinguishable from other cards—it "points." As an example, remove the Ace of Hearts. Orient the card so that the point of the heart is away from you. This card is now "pointing" up. If you rotate the card 180 degrees, the heart will appear upright, pointing in the opposite direction. This is only true of certain cards. The Two of Spades or Ace of Diamonds, for instance, cannot be distinguished upside down or right-side-up due to their symmetry.

1. Remove an assortment of about six pointer cards. Any pointer cards will work, but try to get a balance of colors, values, and suits. Here is the assortment I like to use: Ace of Hearts, Three of Spades (two of the Spades point in the same direction), Five of Hearts (the center Heart pip indicates which way the card points), Five of Clubs (works the same as the Five of Hearts), Nine of Spades (the center Spade pip is directional), and the Seven of Diamonds (the center Diamond pip always favors one end). Here, all six cards point in the same direction (up, or toward the participant).

2. Give your packet a thorough overhand shuffle. If you're feeling bold, you can even ask a spectator to shuffle, miming the actions of an overhand mix. Because the packet is so small, it is unlikely that she will turn cards end for end during the shuffle. The direction of the cards will be maintained.

3. Spread the cards facedown between your hands and ask her to take one from the spread. Let's say she chooses the Seven of Diamonds.

4. Close the spread and say, "I'll turn away so you can look at your card and show it to everybody else." When you turn your back, secretly rotate your packet 180 degrees so it is pointing in the opposite direction.

5. Spread the cards between your hands again and ask the spectator to insert her card back into the spread. Then execute an overhand shuffle (or invite her to shuffle) once more.

Continued 🖝

6. Flip the packet faceup and thumb through the cards one by one, with a pensive look on your face.

7. One card will be pointing in the opposite direction (in this case, the Seven of Diamonds) . . . her selection.

CARD QUIZ

Can you make explosives with playing cards?

Perhaps once upon a time. Decades ago, back when playing cards were made with paper, the red ink on the cards contained diazo dye, which when combined with certain other materials was said to make an explosion.

Author Tom Robbins explains the recipe for a homemade playing card "pow" in *Still Life with Woodpecker*. Moisten and tear up the Hearts and Diamonds until they're mush, and then stuff them into a pipe, plugged at one end. Mix the suits with a household product high in glycerin (Robbins suggests hand lotion) and add potassium permanganate (found in the snakebite section of the first-aid kit under the sink). Plug the pipe and light the thingy on fire. It will explode, shooting a fiery wad out of the end of the pipe!

But cards today aren't explosive as they once were—and tearing up a handful of hearts and diamonds will only succeed in ruining a perfectly good deck of cards!

Barely Lift a Finger

MATERIALS: A deck of playing cards, a thin rubber band **LEVEL:** ♠ ♣ ♦ ♥

In this trick, you locate all four Aces simultaneously simply by lifting your finger. You'll need to prepare the deck in advance, but the execution is dramatic and impressive in its simplicity.

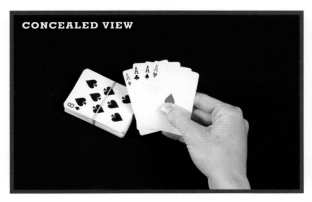

1. In preparation, remove the four Aces and wrap a rubber band around the rest of the deck.

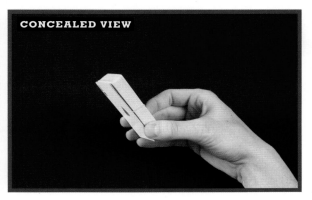

2. Place the Aces on the face of the pack, beneath the wrapped deck. This does require an audience assumption that you begin with a rubber band around the deck.

3. As long as you hold the deck in a Dealers' Grip, the pack will look like it is enveloped by the rubber band.

4. Explain that you will find all four Aces by simply lifting a finger. As you talk, move the right fingers over the deck and grip the upper half by the ends.

Continued ☞

5. Lift the upper half of the cards up and to the right, while still under the wrapped band.

6. Rotate the right hand clockwise, turning the upper packet, causing the rubber band to twist. The upper packet should now be faceup and the rubber band should be tight.

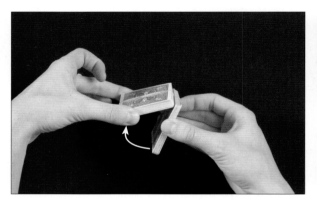

7. Fold the right hand's packet *beneath* the left-hand packet of cards.

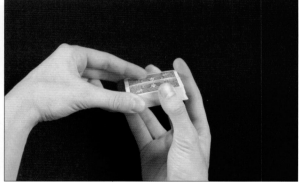

8. Take care to keep the deck square at this point; you don't want to locate the hidden Aces prematurely.

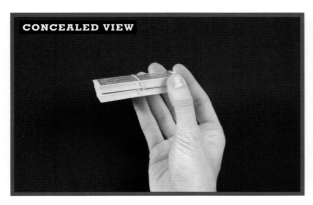

CONCEALED VIEW

9. By cutting the cards in this way, you have tucked the four "unbanded" Aces in the center of an otherwise banded deck.

10. Carefully place the banded deck on the table, all the while keeping the cards square. Readjust so that your right first finger is pressed on top of the deck firmly, keeping all the other cards in alignment.

11. Now for the easy part: locating four Aces by simply lifting a finger. Lift your finger. When you release, the top packet should spin, leaving four cards protruding from the center of the deck.

12. Dramatically remove these cards and display the four Aces to your audience.

Variation: For another spectacular reveal, hide the Aces faceup in Step 2.

Presto Prediction

MATERIALS: Jack of Hearts, Queen of Hearts, King of Hearts, a card box from a standard deck, a scrap of paper, and a permanent marker   **LEVEL: ♠ ♣ ♦ ♥**

Knowing someone's choice before he or she makes it is impossible. It's a lot easier if you cheat! For this trick, you'll use an old magicians' principle called "multiple outs." That is, there are three different endings for the trick, depending on which of the three cards is chosen. Since you will never outline for your participants exactly how the trick will end, the spectators will assume the ending they experience is the only possible outcome.

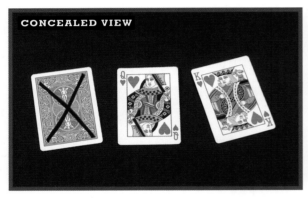

1. On the back of the Jack, draw a large "X" with a permanent marker.

2. On one surface of the card box, write "I knew you would choose the Queen."

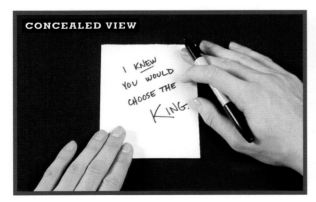

3. Write on a piece of scrap paper "I knew you would choose the King." Then fold the piece of paper.

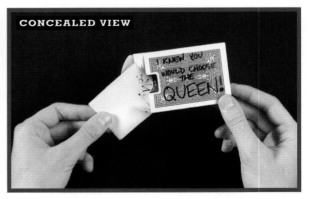

4. To prepare for performance, tuck the prediction inside the card box and place the three cards faceup on top. Then place the box on the table, writing side down. Now go recruit an audience.

5. Address your participant: "Life is about choices. The great aspect of making a decision is that only *you* can make a choice for yourself. But I'm going to prove to you that I already know a choice you will make— and you don't even know it yet." She will be skeptical.

6. Explain that this trick involves just three cards: The Jack, Queen, and King of Hearts. Present the box, taking care to keep the writing out of view. Remove the three cards faceup so as not to expose the X on the back of the Jack. Deal them faceup in a row.

7. "I would like you to choose one of the cards. But don't make it an obvious choice." If the participant is female, for instance, you might point out that she may want to avoid the Queen of Hearts because it would be too obvious, or she may indeed choose the Queen of Hearts because it *is* so obvious, rendering it improbable and thus unlikely to be predicted. Just play games with your participant, talking in circles, until she settles on a card.

8. Hand your participant the card box by gripping it from the sides, and ask her to place the card box on top of the card she has chosen, revealing it for the first time. She will receive the box, gripping it in the same manner that you hold it (which will minimize the chance of prematurely exposing the writing on the box's underside).

Continued ☞

9. The ending depends on which card is chosen—the principle of multiple "outs."

a. **If she places the box on the Jack,** turn over the King and Queen to display nothing written on the backs of the cards. Not impressive . . . yet. Now turn over the Jack of Hearts, revealing an indelible X across its back—an undeniably clear prediction of the participant's choice.

b. **If she places the box on the Queen,** ask her to turn the card box over and read the message intended for her. Another impressive ending.

c. **If she places the box on the King,** open the box and hand her the written prediction. She will read it and wonder how you could have known in advance. (You must remove the prediction from the box yourself and then display the box as empty. If you instruct her to do this, she could possibly discover the other out on the underside of the card box and realize the experiment is fraudulent.)

CARD QUIZ

Were the Kings originally *real* kings?

It depends upon whom you ask. Playing card characters have had so many face-lifts and modifications that their origins are hard to trace. But in the 16th century, playing cards from Paris were modeled after legendary figures from the annals of history. The "Paris" Kings are representative of the four most influential civilizations of pre-medieval culture.

According to some accounts, all the court cards are modeled after distinguished figures in history. The English adapted the costume designs of the ancient Kings to the style of Henry VIII, which accounts for the 15th-century clothing still depicted on cards today. Here is just a sampling of the origins.

The Queen of Hearts may be originally modeled after the Hebrew heroine Judith (what luck—Mom always wanted me to spend time with a nice Jewish girl).

The King of Hearts may represent King Charlemagne of the Holy Roman Empire.

It is suggested that Julius Caesar is depicted on the King of Diamonds to represent the Roman army.

Enter Alexander the Great, King of Macedonia, the man some say is behind the King of Clubs.

The King of Spades may be modeled after King David (as in David and Goliath . . . minus the slingshot).

Friction Four

MATERIALS: A new deck of playing cards   LEVEL: ♠ ♣ ♦ ♥

This instant four-card revelation is a cinch to execute with a crisp new deck. The location of all four Aces happens so fast that they seem to appear at your fingertips in a blur. Just preset the cards (Step 1) and then step right up to the card table.

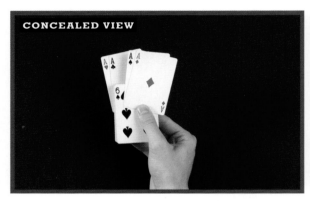

1. Separate the four Aces from the deck and place two on top of the deck and two on the bottom.

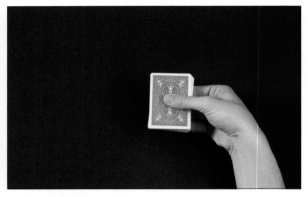

2. Grip the deck facedown with the right thumb on top and the right finger pads below. The thumb should touch only the uppermost Ace and the finger pads only the lowermost Ace.

3. Cock the right wrist to the right and then jerk it sharply to the left, squeezing the top and bottom cards toward each other as you toss the rest of the deck into the awaiting left hand—never letting go with the right hand. In miming the tossing action, you actually release 50 cards into the left hand.

4. All the cards except the top and bottom Ace should have been propelled into the left hand. The upper and lower Ace remain in the right hand. Close your left fingers around the 50 cards using the same grip described in Step 2 with the left thumb above and left finger pads below.

5. In a continuous action, and again squeezing the top and bottom cards (the two remaining Aces) toward each other, toss the cards from your left hand back toward the right so they land across your working surface. *Hint:* While you had to toss the deck with some force to propel it into the other hand in Step 3, don't overdo it when tossing it to the table—the deck should land at least partially squared.

6. The second two Aces remain in the left hand after the tossing action.

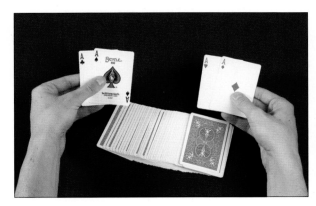

7. At the trick's conclusion, you're left with a pair of cards in each hand. Flip them over in your fingertips to dramatically reveal the four Aces.

A CANCELED DECK

Casinos are the largest buyers and users of playing cards, and regulations allow a pack to be used for only about 8 hours before being exchanged for another. These rigid regulations help curb card tampering. So what happens to all the used decks? Every pack used on a casino table is "cancelled" before it is resold. In the photo below, the pack has been canceled by drilling a hole through its center.

A card cascade is more for show than function, but there are very practical shuffles that are just as elegant.

Chapter 3

Shuffle Bored

Trust your friends, but always cut the cards.

—ANONYMOUS

Sleight of hand has been my passion since I was eight years old: I can shuffle the hell out of a deck of cards. Over the years, I've had countless friends, audience members, and strangers—all embarrassed—ask me to teach them how to shuffle. But like all things in life, there isn't just one answer. There are myriad ways to mix up a pile of playing cards, and you're about to get a comprehensive tutorial.

In recent years, expert card handlers have elevated this simple task to an intricate art form. And beware the magician's shuffle: There's a good chance the shuffle isn't really mixing the cards (this is called a false shuffle). Casino shuffles, fancy flourishes, false cuts—it's all here. Even if you think you're a master mixer, much of what you're about to read will be new to you.

Hindu Shuffle

MATERIALS: A deck of playing cards   **LEVEL:** ♠ ♣ ♦ ♥

Magicians call this unusual way of mixing cards the Hindu shuffle, but it is by no means exclusive. When I was on tour in Asia doing magic shows, I found this way of mixing the standard. I guarantee none of your poker buddies mixes cards like this—you'll be the life of the party.

1. Begin by holding the deck at the sides, facedown between your right thumb and finger pads. As shown, the finger pads contact the deck at the inner edge, which allows the left fingers to access the front of the deck more easily.

2. Move your left hand underneath the deck, approaching it palm up.

3. Wrap the left fingers around the pack, pinching the top edges of the deck at the sides with the pads of your thumb and second finger.

4. Using these two fingers as pincers, grasp a small packet of cards (8 to 10 cards) and break them from the rest of the deck by lifting up slightly with the left hand.

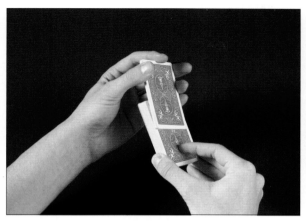

5. Slide the left hand forward, away from your body, until the packet of cards in the left hand clears the rest of the deck.

6. Release the left second finger and thumb's grip on the packet, allowing it to fall into a rest position on the left palm.

7. In a continuing action, approach the deck with the left hand, again from beneath, but this time with the addition of holding a packet. Don't let this packet of cards distract you; it doesn't affect the mechanics of the shuffle. Repeat the actions in Steps 2–4, taking another small packet between the pads of the second finger and thumb. The growing packet that rests on the left palm will not interfere with the move.

8. Again, slide the left hand forward and release the packet held between the left middle finger and thumb . . .

Continued 👉

9. . . . allowing it to pile on top of the first packet.

10. Continue shuffling in this manner until the entire deck has been transferred to the left hand. Then repeat. Concentrate on speed and neatness; it's important to take the packets *cleanly* into the left hand or the shuffle will look inelegant.

THE POWER OF THE FORCE

Magicians sometimes use the Hindu shuffle you just learned for more devious practices: forcing a card. The same mechanics can be used to force a predetermined card on an unsuspecting spectator. She will believe her choice is random, but you will secretly know the identity of her card.

It's easy to learn. You must first secretly ascertain the identity of the bottom card of the deck; this will be the card you force. Then execute the Hindu shuffle as described, taking small packets of cards into your left hand. Ask a spectator to call "stop" any time she wishes. When stopped, separate your hands and raise the packet in your right hand, holding the face of the bottom card toward the spectator. Even though the bottom card doesn't change during the Hindu shuffle, the illusion of stopping randomly on this card is quite convincing.

How do you use this force? There are lots of ways, but here is an excellent one. After the force, bury the card and put away the deck. Say, *"We won't even use the deck. Just stare into my eyes and think of the name of your card . . ."* Now cock an eyebrow, take a deep breath, and announce the name of your force card.

Tabled Riffle Shuffle

MATERIALS: A deck of playing cards, a soft table surface   LEVEL: ♠♣♦♥

One of the most important differences between man and other species is the opposable thumb, which allows man to both overhand and riffle shuffle.

—Steve Beam, *Semi-Automatic Card Tricks, Volume 2*

Did you ever wonder why cards are always mixed with riffle shuffles in Las Vegas? Nevada state regulations. For the protection of both the players and the casinos, the cards are given tidy, tabled riffle shuffles. The tabled riffle shuffle's actions are compact and precise, rendering it difficult to catch a glimpse or secretly note the value of a card during a shuffle. With a casual overhand shuffle or a mix in the hands, the bottom card in the deck is usually exposed to at least one other player. Shuffles that involve a large riffling action risk exposing cards near the top as they are riffled off the thumb. The riffle shuffle makes it difficult for the peeled eyes of poker players and even the occasional crooked dealer. A soft working surface is essential for this shuffle. Although you don't need casino-green felt, it definitely adds atmosphere.

1. Begin with the deck facedown on the table, oriented sideways, as shown, and just left of your body's center point.

2. With the right thumb and fingers, cut approximately half the deck to the right. Place the cut-off packet ½ inch from the lower half, so that only a minimal amount of movement is necessary to weave the cards.

Continued 🖝

3. Both hands will mirror each other from this point. Place your thumbs on the sides of the packets closest to you, just shy of the packets' centers.

4. The first fingers rest, curled, on top of the packets while the second and ring fingers brace the packets at the opposite sides. The little finger of each hand keeps the outer end of each packet squared.

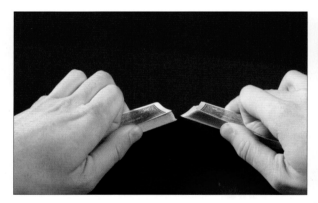

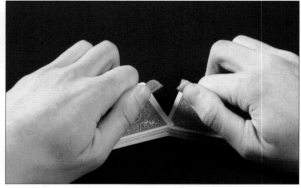

5. Lift the thumbs slightly, raising the inner corners of each packet. After both corners have been raised, both hands move (each as a unit) toward each other so that the cards' corners overlap.

6. Riffle cards slowly and simultaneously off each thumb, allowing the cards to weave at *only* the inner corner. *Hint:* Think soft and gentle; very little pressure is required to weave playing cards.

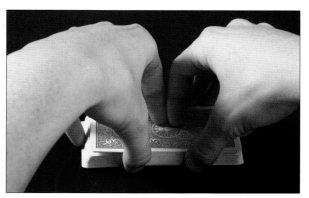

7. After all the cards have been riffled off the thumbs, straighten the little finger of each hand.

8. Move your hands together to square the cards, keeping each packet square against the flexed little fingers. The flexed little fingers brace the packets from the ends and help the cards slide together. Now you're ready to shuffle cards in Vegas.

A FLUID RIFFLE

If you're having trouble doing the riffle shuffle fluidly, your grip is still too firm. Martin A. Nash, a close-up card magician known as the "Charming Cheat," gave a demonstration to emphasize the importance of gentle shuffling. He would open a brand-new deck of cards and ruin it in three casual shuffles. They aren't obnoxious shuffles; they are just firm, tense riffle shuffles. He purposely applied too much thumb pressure and held the cards too firmly as he riffled, causing the corners to bend and bow. After just three shuffles like this, the pack is worthless to a card handler. A gentle shuffle will save you aggravation and money.

In-the-Hands Riffle Shuffle

MATERIALS: A deck of playing cards   LEVEL: ♠ ♣ ♦ ♥

Playing cards are addictive, and if I've done my job, you'll be toting them around with you everywhere (you know you're dedicated when there are spare packs in the glove box and bathroom). But in many of the places where you'll have cards, you'll be lacking a surface to put them on. This shuffle, also called a Dovetail Shuffle, is one I use all the time because it involves no table. If you're ever playing Spades in an airport or practicing your One-Handed Fans in a waiting room, this is your weapon of choice.

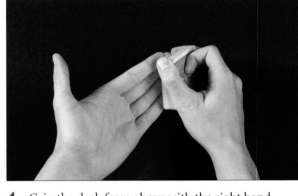

1. Grip the deck from above with the right hand. Curl the first finger on top of the deck so that the first and second knuckles rest on the top card.

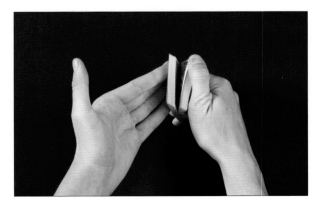

2. Rotate the right hand so the thumb is uppermost. The left finger pads should be positioned on the face of the deck.

3. Riffle approximately half the cards off the right thumb onto the awaiting left fingers. Insert the left thumb into the break between the packets and grip the lower packet between the left thumb and fingers.

4. You can now separate the hands as each hand grips half the pack independently.

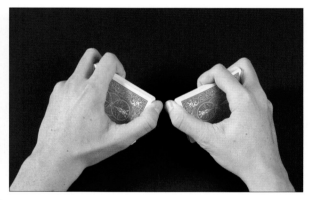

5. The right hand's grip on its packet is already correct, so no adjustments are necessary. Regrip the left packet, however, with the left thumb at one end and the fingers at the other. The grip and action of both hands should mirror each other.

6. You'll note that the packets are in a deep grip in each hand. That is, the outer end of each packet is aligned with the base of the fingers. Wrap the first fingers around their respective packets, allowing the pad of each first finger to contact the face card of each packet. The positioning of the first finger helps brace the packets from beneath (in lieu of a table).

Continued ☞

7. To execute the shuffle, riffle the cards in each packet off the thumbs, allowing them to weave together. Notice that in this shuffle, unlike the riffle shuffle, the entire ends of the packets overlap.

8. Use your fingers to gently push the card packets flush. It can and should be repeated, ad nauseum. Look, Ma, no table!

CARD QUIZ

Have playing cards saved lives?

Yes! In 1943, the U.S. Playing Card Company began a secret project with the U.S. government. It printed small maps (scale: 1:100,000) indicating escape routes on the inside layer of playing cards. These cards were shipped to German POW camps as medical parcels or "donations." American prisoners could secretly soak these cards until the glue dissolved and the layers of the cards could be peeled apart. Reassembled as a full map, the cards would show suggested exit routes—which were used by prisoners in several successful escapes.

Today, the U.S. Playing Card edition is exceedingly rare.

Overhand Shuffle

MATERIALS: A deck of playing cards   **LEVEL:** ♠ ♣ ♦ ♥

No shuffling lesson would be complete without a tutorial on the venerable overhand shuffle; it's a rite of passage in most private games. But this shuffle is easily corruptible, so be mindful of its pitfalls (see sidebar, page 64). It should be noted that the overhand shuffle isn't thorough; it merely displaces large groups of cards, which is only one step above a solitary "cut." When money is on the line, do like the casino dealers and use more than one method of shuffling.

1. Grip the facedown deck from the bottom in your right hand, fingers at the outer end and thumb at the inner end. Angle your hand so the pack is at a 45-degree angle to the ground.

2. Move your left fingers under the pack as you rest the left thumb on top of the uppermost card.

Continued ☞

3. With your right finger and thumb pads, ease your grip on the uppermost 10 or so cards as the left thumb applies pressure on top of the deck. Allow this upper packet of cards to fall into the cradle of the awaiting left fingers.

4. Immediately repeat this action, sliding a small number of cards from the top of the right-hand packet and allowing them to fall onto the left-hand packet.

ON DEFENSE

This book earns you a master's degree in shuffling, but invariably some guy will use the overhand shuffle in a game you're involved in (not everyone has the benefit of a higher shuffling education). You'll need to watch for two things when others use this shuffle. First, if the deck isn't held at a 45-degree angle, the bottom card will be exposed. Knowing the bottom card is an unfair advantage. Second, by taking only one card off the top at the beginning of the shuffle, this card will go immediately to the bottom (where an able cheat will deal it to himself or an accomplice using a bottom deal). And finally, while it may sound obvious, doing a faceup overhand shuffle should set off alarm bells in your head. Any capable cheat watching will likely know the identity and order of the top few cards, which is enough information to take the rest of the players for an expensive ride.

5. Repeat this action until you have transferred all of the cards from the right hand into the left.

Faro Shuffle

MATERIALS: A deck of playing cards   LEVEL: ♠ ♣ ♦ ♥

You're about to learn the most precise shuffle in the world. Several books have been written about the Perfect Faro Shuffle, the mathematics involved, and tricks that utilize it. You will perfectly weave two packets together. That is, the cards will alternate evenly between the packets. When you're proficient, it takes less than two seconds to weave all 52 cards—it takes considerably longer to master this skill.

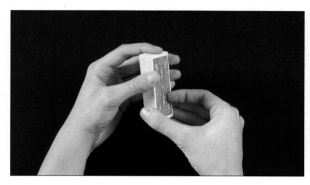

1. Hold the deck facedown between the left thumb and finger pads, gripped on the sides toward the upper end of the pack. Curl the left first finger pad around the upper end of the deck. Move your right hand toward the left and grip the cards in much the same way: Situate the right thumb below the left thumb and place the right finger pads on the deck just below the left finger pads.

2. With your right thumb, riffle approximately halfway into the deck.

3. Break the deck at this point, taking the upper portion into your right hand.

4. Move the outer end of the right hand's half below the left hand's packet, and butt the ends together.

Continued 👉

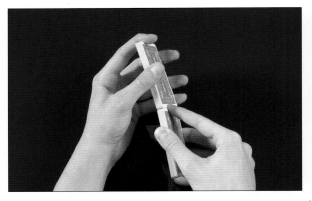

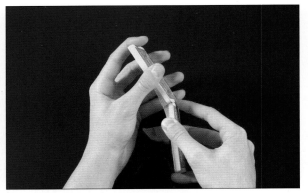

5. To keep both card packets square, extend the right first finger to the juncture between the packets and apply pressure.

6. To carry out the shuffle, push the packets together, applying more pressure to the inner side where the packets meet. Slide the upper, left-hand packet toward your body slightly, scraping it against the lower packet. These actions cause the first few inner cards to weave between each other.

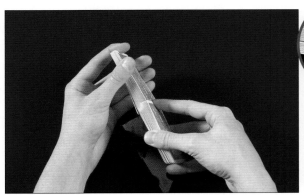

7. When this happens, simply increase the pressure *slightly*. Like a zipper, the rest of the deck should follow suit. It can be tricky to start, but once the process begins, the cards weave seamlessly. The mechanics of starting the shuffle will vary depending on the condition of your cards, the humidity, and luck. Experiment with tiny movements of the left and right hand and different degrees of pressure to find what works best in each situation.

8. Assess: You may notice small imperfections in the shuffle (marked above), where two cards from the same packet remained together. With practice, you can get a perfect weave without these flaws. You may also notice a large block of cards on the top or bottom of a particular packet. This just means you didn't cut exactly 26 cards in each packet.

Variations: Most of you can live a fulfilled life without ever attempting a perfect faro shuffle. A normal faro is a thorough, silent way of mixing cards. However, if you do decide to learn perfect faro shuffles, here are three challenges.

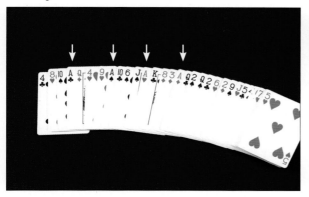

■ **Stacking Four Aces:** Place four Aces on top of the pack and give it two in-faro shuffles ("in" means that the original top card, in this case an Ace, becomes the second card from the top after the shuffle). After the second in-faro, the Aces will be stacked for a four-handed game of poker so that each one falls to you, the dealer.

■ **Perfect Giant Fan:** Now that you know the faro shuffle, revisit the Giant Fan (page 19). You will be able to do it much faster, and it looks markedly better with this extra bit of panache.

FOLLOWING THE SHUFFLE

While it may sound difficult, magicians often rely on a perfect faro shuffle (see page 68). That is, we learn to split the deck at exactly the halfway point (26 cards in each packet) and then weave the cards perfectly. When done with this kind of precision, there's a world of possibilities. If you know a particular card's location, you can calculate its new location after the shuffle (for the curious, it's the card's current position multiplied by two, minus one . . . not that you asked).

If you do eight perfect faros in a row, you'll return the deck to the order it started in. Just make sure you do eight perfect "out" faro shuffles, which means at each shuffle's completion, the top and bottom cards remain the same.

ONE-HANDED FARO SHUFFLE

Playing cards have the ability to cloud men's minds, or to dominate them.

—RICKY JAY, *in* Playing Cards *by Donald Sultan*

Fewer than a hundred people worldwide can execute a perfect, one-handed shuffle. It involves splitting the cards at exactly 26 and 26, aligning the edges, and then lightly pressing the edges together so that every card alternates. Perfect shuffles, with one or two hands, have fascinating mathematical potential. Eight perfect out-Faro shuffles restores the deck to its starting order. If four Aces are placed on top of the deck, after two perfect shuffles, the Aces will be positioned every fourth card, stacked for a four-handed game. How does the old saying go? Trust your friends, but always cut the cards.

The Bridge

MATERIALS: A deck of playing cards   **LEVEL:** ♠ ♣ ♦ ♡

Whether you use a faro or a riffle shuffle, a bridge is a classy way to assemble the cards. After the cards have been woven but before they have been squared, try this classy flourish. And for those who can already perform a bridge, skip to the double bridge to learn something you've never seen.

1. For the classic card bridge, begin in a position where the ends of the deck have been woven. A faro shuffle (page 65) works ideally here because the weave is so thorough. You can also start an in-the-hands shuffle (page 60). Make sure the cards overlap about 1 inch.

2. Hold this extended "telescoped" pack horizontally, facedown between your hands, with the fingers supporting it from beneath and the thumbs resting on top. Apply pressure between the thumb and fingers of each hand to keep the cards in position.

3. With the deck in this clamped position, roll your wrists away from each other, causing the telescoped deck to bow. The finger pads continue to apply pressure below the bowed deck.

4. Make sure that the cards don't prematurely "spring" together during the bowing action, and position the thumbs at the apex of the bridge.

5. To execute the bridge, flatten the fingers beneath the telescoped pack.

6. The flattening of the fingers allows the cards from each packet to spring toward each other. With the thumb pads, push on the top of the deck to keep cards from flying out of your hands. This flourish can't be done slowly.

THE JOKER

The evolution of the Joker card is erroneously attributed to the fool card in a tarot deck. Actually, this iconic card first appeared in 1865 in the game of *euchre,* a popular game among German-American immigrants. In this game, the most powerful card is the Jack of the Trump suit, referred to as the "best bower." In 1865, American cardmaker Samuel Hart created a special best bower card to replace the Jack. This card was named after the game its bearer would win: the euchre card. And "euchre" in German is *jucker.* Although euchre's popularity was replaced by poker, the *jucker,* or Joker, remains.

The Double Bridge

MATERIALS: A deck of playing cards   LEVEL: ♠ ♣ ♦ ♥

Bridging cards is standard fare at poker tables worldwide. But bridging cards twice separates the men from the boys.

1. The double bridge begins in the same position as the bridge (page 70), gripping the telescoped pack with both hands. But, for the double bridge, it's essential that you use a faro shuffle to mix the cards. Place the partially shuffled deck in your left hand, gripping the pack where both packets are interlaced about 1 inch.

2. Move your right hand above the telescoped pack. Place your right second finger pad at the outer right corner of the outer packet and your right thumb pad on the inner left corner of the inner packet.

3. Apply pressure at these opposite corners of the telescoped pack. That is, bow the elongated deck upward as you apply diagonal pressure (see arrows).

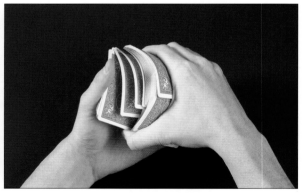

4. Relax the pressure with your fingers, allowing the cards from each packet to spring toward each other. However, because the cards spring in slightly different directions, the packets remain segregated. That is, the outer packet gathers to the left of the inner packet.

5. If you examine it closely, you'll see that although the packets are now square at the ends, they remain separated at the sides.

6. For the second bridge, regrip the deck from beneath with the palm-up left hand. The right hand supports the deck from above.

7. Bow the deck in a concave manner and then slowly release the pressure with your right index finger.

8. The cards will bridge again, this time from their sidestepped position.

9. At the conclusion, you'll be holding the deck squared in the left hand, ready to deal.

False Cut

MATERIALS: A deck of playing cards, a table surface   LEVEL: ♠ ♣ ♦ ♥

Who would want to learn how *not* to mix cards? A cheater—that's who. In a game of cards, stacking the deck is only half the battle. Once the deck is stacked, the cheater must maintain his arrangement while giving the impression that the cards are being mixed. While we've already learned several ways of shuffling and cutting cards, this move merely simulates a cut. Actually, the order of the cards after the move is exactly the same as in the beginning. The key to this cut, popularized by magician Jay Ose, is all rhythm. As long as the cards are cut and then assembled in one slow, fluid sequence, it will look like a genuine triple cut. I'm certainly not suggesting you cheat at cards, but if you ever *do* go to the trouble of stacking a deck, I'd hate to see you accidentally shuffle away your winning hand. Basically, you'll be cutting the deck into three piles and then assembling those piles in the same order you cut them. Net effect: nothing.

1. Hold the deck in your left hand. Begin by cutting approximately a third of the deck with the right hand and placing it on the table, to your right.

2. Next, cut another third and place it to the left of the first packet.

3. Finally, take the remaining third of the deck into the right hand and place it on the table to the left of the other two packets.

4. With the right hand, scoop up the rightmost packet and plop it on top of the center packet.

5. Take the combined packet and slap it on top of the leftmost, bottom packet. Done in one fluid rhythm, it really looks like you've given the deck a triple cut.

CARD QUIZ

Shuffling cards is cool. But what is _un_shuffling?

Unshuffling or "sorting" cards involves putting a shuffled pack back into order (Ace through King or King through Ace, segregated by suits). The current world record for sorting a pack of cards is 36.1 seconds, held by the Czech Republic's Zdeněk Bradáč.

 Sorting cards is a growing industry. As of December 2000, the Warm Springs Correctional Center in Nevada introduced a card-sorting program for its inmates. Thirty inmates are selected to sort cancelled casino playing cards so they can be resold. We know that fast hands with a pack of cards can get you locked up, but apparently that's a skill worth having on the inside.

Trust your friends, but *always* cut the cards.

Chapter 4

Cheap Tricks & Safe Bets

A deck of cards is the perfect tool for deceit.

—David Britland and Gazzo, *Phantoms of the Card Table*

Seventeenth-century clergymen (not exactly my target audience) referred to playing cards as "The Devil's prayer book" or "The Devil's picture book," and outlawed them

because they could be—and were—used as tools for deception. My, things have changed. Cards in and of themselves are fairly innocent instruments—they're mere illustrations on cardboard, after all. It's what the card handler does with them that gives them the power to save lives, win fortunes, solve crimes, or (gulp) draw blood. But rest assured, you can use every prank featured in this chapter with almost no risk of being burned at the stake.

Fake Marked Cards

MATERIALS: A deck of playing cards   **LEVEL:** ♠ ♣ ♦ ♥

Being caught using marked cards isn't funny unless you enjoy life without the use of opposable thumbs. But accusing someone else of using marked cards can be hilarious. Every poker game has one insufferable player—you know, the one who clouds up your basement with cigar smoke and eats all the salsa. Just remember, the bigger he is, the harder he falls. *Note:* I hate stating the obvious, but be sure to use someone else's deck for this. Proving that you can read the marks on *your* cards is counterproductive and, depending on your opponents, dangerous.

1. Between rounds, when it's your turn to shuffle, act as though you've been offended. "What's going on here? These cards are marked!" Spread through the cards, studying the backs carefully. Draw on your best acting abilities because, obviously, the cards aren't actually marked. Look at the person winning most frequently and accuse the poor sucker of marking the deck. He will squirm in his chair and turn redder than the King of Hearts.

2. Offer to explain. To prove the cards are marked, ask someone to shuffle the cards and then cut off a packet of about 10 cards.

3. Take the packet and spread through it facedown, shaking your head and feigning disappointment: "Really? Marked cards? I thought we were friends." Square the packet and hold it in your right hand by the ends, fingers above and thumb below.

4. Hold the packet with the faces toward the audience at chest height. Bow the cards (so they arc toward you) by squeezing the fingers and thumb toward each other.

5. Interestingly, if the cards are held in this position at the right height, you should be able to clearly see the face card's index at the lower left corner. Remember this card—let's say it's the Five of Spades.

6. Using the left finger pads, slide the face card into the left hand. Hold the card normally in the left hand so you cannot possibly see the face. Now that you're in a position where you can't see its identity, stare intently at the card, as if reading the marks on its back. Shout out its name, which you already know (in this case, the Five of Spades).

Continued 👉

7. Before you peel the new face card from the right hand's packet with your left fingers, glimpse the identity of the new face card as you did in Step 5 by bending the cards as described above. For variation (shown), you can also glimpse the face card of the packet in your right hand under cover of a pointing gesture: Before dropping the card in your left hand, point to a spot on the back of it with your right first finger. Say, "I can see the mark right there," and point to any spot on the back of the card in the left hand. As you point, bend the right packet as explained and catch a glimpse of the next card.

8. Then slide the face card from the right hand into the left, stare at the back of the card for a few seconds, and then call out its value and suit. Repeat this stunt until either you run out of cards or the other players declare mob rule.

DON'T GET CAUGHT

How can you spot a marked deck?

The riffle test probably originated on gambling riverboats in the 1800s, and it's still the best test for finding marks. Holding the deck facedown in your left hand, riffle the end of the deck upward like a flipbook. If the deck is marked, you'll see flowers, angels, and whatever else that has been altered come to life, as dots and blocked-out petals dance across the backs of the cards. Gamblers call this "going to the movies."

There exists another kind of marking, not detectable by the riffle test. "Juice" decks are a different marking system entirely, and one that is easier to spot from far away than with close inspection. The idea is to coat an area of a card with a faint trace of "juice," a diluted ink solution that casts a shadowy red or blue (depending on the color of the back design) over certain areas. Juice decks are used primarily so that a cheat can determine high cards from low cards.

HOFZINSER CARD

"Playing cards are the poetry of magic," magician Johann Hofzinser (1806–1875) once said. Hofzinser was the brain behind a fascinating gaffed card that had been all but forgotten until recently.

You already know that a playing card is comprised of three layers (see page 43). Hofzinser altered the middle layer of a card. When this card was placed in front of a candle, backside out, the candle would eliminate the pips on the innermost card. But when the card was turned around (and moved away from the candle), it would be seen to change to another card.

Lit from behind while spotlighting only a corner from the front allows you to see the card, and at the same time see through it.

Memorizing a Deck

MATERIALS: A deck of playing cards   LEVEL: ♠ ♣ ♦ ♥

To make your buddies think you memorized an entire deck of cards (which they can shuffle beforehand), you actually only need to remember one card and count from 1 to about 20.

1. Announce that you will memorize a deck of cards after another player has shuffled it. Hand out the deck to be shuffled. As she completes the mixing, secretly remember the bottom card of the deck. If the card isn't visible, take the deck back and look at the bottom card. Let's assume it's the Three of Clubs (magicians call this a "key" card).

2. Holding the deck of cards in your left hand, invite the participant to cut off a packet and instruct her to hold it in her hand.

CARD QUIZ

Can people *really* memorize a shuffled deck of cards?

Amazingly, yes! On November 3, 1994, Tom Groves memorized a shuffled deck of cards in 42.01 seconds without a single error. But rumor has it that after the event, he couldn't remember where he parked. On November 26, 1993, Dominic O'Brien memorized 40 decks of cards (2,080 cards total) in a single sighting with only one mistake, setting the world record (for memorizing cards, not mistakes).

3. Now ask the participant to look at the card on top of the packet still in *your* hand—the card she cut to—and remember it.

4. After she commits the card to memory, ask her to place her selected card on top of the pile in her hands.

5. To apparently bury the card, plop the packet in your hand on top of her cards. The card appears buried somewhere in the deck, but it's actually right next to your key card on the bottom of the deck, in this case, the Three of Clubs.

6. Take the deck back and spread through the cards quickly with the faces toward you. Using your best acting skills, act as if you are memorizing every card as it goes by. In truth, you're spreading through the cards until you find the key card, the Three of Clubs. The card to its immediate right is the spectator's card, but you don't even have to remember it. Instead, just count every remaining card, starting with the selection, until you reach the end of the deck.

Continued ☞

7. Let's assume the selection is 16th from the top. Turn the deck facedown, hand it to your friend, or smack it facedown on the table and announce, "I just memorized the entire deck!"

8. Ask the participant which card she picked. Once she answers, pretend to concentrate intently, as if trying to recall the position of the selected card. After the appropriate period of head-scratching, tell everyone that the card just named is at the 16th position (or whatever number) from the top. Allow the participant to deal the cards one at a time. When she reaches 15, stop her for a moment.

9. "If I'm correct, the 15th card should be the Three of Clubs, and the next one should be yours." Here, as an added touch, you merely call out the name of your key card when you reach its position, just before the selection. By calling out this card at its position in addition to the selected card, the implication is that you really did memorize every card in the deck. Allow her to deal the last card and turn it faceup, "proving" that you memorized an entire deck of cards.

10. Now would be a good time to shuffle the cards before some jerk starts quizzing you on the order of the other cards.

Getting Mental

MATERIALS: A deck of playing cards, a friend, a table surface   LEVEL: ♠♣♦♥

Reading a person's thoughts is impossible, but your friends will swear you have telepathic abilities after this stunt.

You will communicate the identity of the chosen card through a secret code known only to you and your accomplice. I've designed the code so that it is easy to remember and therefore easy to teach someone on the spot or at the bar—this "sixth sense" mystique stuff goes over great at parties.

Here's the scenario, as your spectators will see it. Your friend, the "receiver," will leave the room while a card is selected. Once the receiver is gone, you'll ask someone to think of a card. When the receiver returns, you'll look each other in the eyes with your fingers on your temples, apparently sending the thought of the card. After a brief mental struggle, the receiver can correctly name the chosen card.

1. Your friend (accomplice) leaves the room. You take the cards from the box and table the box at the center of your working surface. This will function as a visual guide to your friend.

2. A participant selects a card, say the King of Spades.

Continued ☞

3. Think of the table as the face of a clock and the box as the clock's center (no hands on this clock, of course). The value of the chosen card is coded by where you place the pack of cards in relation to the box.

a. If it's directly to the box's right, it's 3:00—and the chosen card is a Three.

b. Slightly higher, at the 2:00 position, and the selected card is a Two.

c. Below the box and slightly to the left is 7:00, which means the spectator chose a Seven.

d. Cards directly to the left of the card box indicate a Nine, and so on.

e. Jack is 11:00 since the Jack's worth is 11.

f. Queen is represented by the 12:00 position.

4. There is no hour equivalent for the King, which in this case, was the participant's selection. For a King, simply place the cards on top of the box.

5. This stunt can be repeated ad nauseum, but to throw off anyone watching for patterns, you can vary the distance of the pack from the box; that is, the cards are still placed in the correct time zones, but the appearance changes. *Example:* You may code a chosen Three by placing the pack an inch from the box and the next time you might code a Three by placing the deck two feet away from its box.

6. After the card has been chosen and you've noted the number or face and suit, shuffle the card back into the deck and table it in its proper place. Ask someone to retrieve your friend.

Continued ☞

7. A quick glance at the table will tell your friend the value (deck on box = King) of the chosen card, but the suit remains a mystery. The suit is coded with the first letter of the first word of the first sentence you say to her. There are four suits in a deck: Hearts, Clubs, Spades, and Diamonds, or H, C, S, and D. You'll invite the receiver to interpret your thoughts in one of four ways:

■ Hearts: "Here, try this one" or "Have a go at this."

■ Clubs: "Can you give this a try?" "Close your eyes and concentrate."

■ Spades: "See if you can guess Jon's card" or "Stop right there. What card am I thinking of?"

■ Diamonds: "Do you know what card Mary thought of?" or "Don't worry about everyone else, just concentrate on the card."

Since the chosen card's suit is Spades, your verbal cue must start with the letter S.

8. Psychology and acting are of equal importance here. Even though your friend will know the identity of the chosen card within seconds of entering the room, she must feign struggle before revealing the card. Your acting is important, too. Look her in the eye and squint—sending thoughts would be a draining process, right?

You can also enhance this scam verbally. Always try to reiterate that the cards are truly chosen at random by the participants. "See if you can guess the card Mike thought of." From your wording, it sounds as if your friend might even be intercepting Mike's thoughts—a feat more impressive than reading just one person's mind. "Come here. Angela thought of a card and she *swears* she didn't tell you. What card is she thinking of?"

9. By diverting all the attention to Angela, many viewers will forget you even saw the card, making it all the more amazing when your friend correctly identifies the randomly thought-of card: the King of Spades.

Flipped

MATERIALS: A deck of playing cards, a table surface   LEVEL: ♠ ♣ ♦ ♥

Many of the sleights and ruses that magicians use to dazzle were originally used to deceive. Flipped can be used to amaze or confound, depending on whether you present it as magic or a con. Below, you'll explore how best to exploit the principle as a bet. But fear not, you can't lose.

CONCEALED VIEW

1. Secretly note the bottom card of your deck—con men call this a "key" card.

2. Approach a guy with an obtuse look on his face—con men call guys like this "marks." Ask him to cut the cards and place the cut-off portion in your hand.

3. Ask him to remember the card he cut to, pointing to the packet on the table. Let's say it's the Two of Clubs.

4. Ask the mark to replace the card on top of the cards in your hand.

Continued ☞

5. Then ask him to complete the cut by placing the tabled packet on top of everything. While it appears that the mark cut the deck, looked at a card, and then buried it, his selection actually rests just below the card you remembered at the outset. You have complete control over the card, and he hasn't got a clue.

6. Begin dealing the cards in a faceup pile. Instruct your participant not to indicate if you pass his card—you'll find it without any help. This is all smoke; you know exactly where his card is. Deal with relative speed, all the while watching for the key card. When you deal the key card faceup, it's time to pay close attention.

7. Without breaking rhythm, deal the participant's selection faceup *and then two more cards.* You want to give the impression that you've unknowingly botched the demonstration.

8. Take the next card facedown in the right hand and stare at it intently. "The next card I turn over will be your card. Do you want to wager against that?" The circumstances are extraordinary: The odds of actually finding the right card are 1 in 52. The mark has also seen his card go onto the pile of discards, so he can be sure the card in the right hand is not his—and it's not. He won't be able to get to his wallet fast enough.

9. Whatever he offers to bet, hesitate for a moment, as if it's too much, but ultimately agree to as much as he is willing to bet—at least the tab on your next drink. To win the bet, place the card in your right hand facedown on the table.

10. Spread over the top two indifferent cards on the discard pile, exposing the participant's selection.

11. Pick up the card so your participant can see, and turn it facedown.

12. You win, game over. Remind him that you said "The next card I turn over will be your card." The next card you turned over really was his card. Sometimes ambiguity pays off; it just paid for your drink.

❧ SHINERS ❧

Fortunately, we know what cheats are up to. At least, we think we do.

—David Britland and Gazzo, *Phantoms of the Card Table*

Shiners (cheaters call them "glims" or "twinkles") are hidden mirrors that secretly reflect the identities of facedown cards to the dealer. Cheaters have hidden mirrors in virtually any object you might find at the card table: on or in a ring (below), a watch, glasses, the end of a cigarette, and even the inside of a pipe (below, right). And the technology is getting even sleeker. A shiner was recently uncovered within a playing card (right), secreted by a folding flap. Today, the most common form of a shiner is an upturned cell phone. At the right angle, in the right light, the screen gives off a perfect reflection of cards sailing from the dealer's hands, passing above the phone's screen.

Shiners render most marked decks obsolete because they can be used at any time with any deck. For the cheater, it's like playing with the cards faceup.

A very crooked deal.

Last Words

Playing cards are a survival of our less rational, more frightful, more beautiful past.

—DAVID MAMET, in *Playing Cards* by Donald Sultan

hen I look at playing cards, I see limitless potential. When these simple symbols are shuffled, fortunes are won, the future is foretold, or magic is unleashed.

Cards can be used for self-defense or to separate a sucker from his money. They personify our innate obsession with chance, and they reward our strategic cunning. The cards themselves are relics of ancient times and craft, and their history is forever intertwined with ours. Whether it's the World Series of Poker or a child seeing his first magic trick, lives can change with the turn of a card. I've enjoyed sharing my quirky collection of "cardistry" with you, and I hope these stunts are as fun for you to do as they have been for me to invent, practice, and describe. Playing cards are my obsession; they have taken me all over the world and exposed me to fascinating people and unforgettable experiences. For these reasons and more, I'm equally indebted to the cards and to you.

Take care, and take cards.

— JOSHUA JAY
New York City

Appendix

Further Reading

The world of playing cards is fragmented, but it is full of generous, inventive people. The only prerequisite for participating in any of these organizations is a love for playing cards and the ability to do eight perfect one-handed faro shuffles. I'm kidding about that last part.

For Card Tricks

If you liked the card tricks and flourishes in the pages of this book, let me make three recommendations to you.

1. Join a magic society. There's no better path to becoming a great magician than joining a fraternal organization. Magicians meet for lectures, conventions, and monthly gatherings (these are not as dorky as they sound; in fact, they're quite fun). The two biggest U.S.-based magic organizations are:

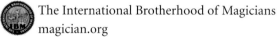 The International Brotherhood of Magicians
magician.org

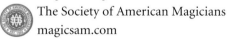 The Society of American Magicians
magicsam.com

2. Check out *Magic: The Complete Course,* written by me, and brought to you by the same kind folks who published the book and DVD you're holding. This is the magic book and DVD I wish I'd had when I started.
It's equal parts presentation and technique, and between the covers are over a hundred professional-caliber magic

tricks you can do. For card lovers, there's a chapter called "The Ten Greatest Card Tricks of All Time."

3. If you like flourishes (fans, fancy cuts, etc.), check out dananddave.com. Dan and Dave Buck are twins who have, in essence, started a new movement with card flourishes. These guys shuffle cards with superhuman agility, and they have a burgeoning online community to support this creative and exciting new trend.

For Card History

If playing-card history or collecting is your thing, allow me to make three more suggestions:

1. Join the International Playing-Card Society. Based in the U.K. but with membership all over the world, this is the best way to learn about the history of playing cards and how to view the best collections all over the world. i-p-c-s.org

2. Next time you're in Paris, visit Le Musée Français de la Carte à Jouer, a stunning museum with an unrivaled display of cards of every shape and design. You'll have a new appreciation for cards as works of art: issy.com/statiques/musee/

3. Read *Roll the Bones: The History of Gambling* by David G. Schwartz. This is a much overdue modern tome on the colorful history of gambling. It also covers the most modern developments concerning the origins of playing cards.

Playing-Card History: Playing cards have a rich history and industry, yet there is no generally accepted consensus on some of the most fundamental questions. The brief glimpses into the origins and trivia of playing cards have been gleaned from numerous sources, people, and experiences. Some notable titles:

A History of Playing Cards and a Bibliography of Cards and Gaming, by Catherine Perry Hargrave, 1930, Dover Reprint Edition.

For Cheaters and Cons

Finally, for those of you fascinated by the underworld of cheaters, mechanics, con men, and advantage play, here are three exhilarating *true* tales that center around a pack of cards:

1. *The Magician and the Cardsharp* by Karl Johnson, 2005, Henry Holt Books. This book chronicles the obsession of magic's greatest card expert, Dai Vernon. He became obsessed with the elusive center deal sleight and its fabled practitioner. His journey eventually brought him to the unlikeliest of places and the sketchiest of cheaters.

2. *Phantoms of the Card Table* by David Britland and Gazzo, 2003, High Stakes Publishing. This book, which also deals with Dai Vernon (it's hard to write about the subject *without* including the guy), surveys many of the most colorful characters who shuffled cards, and also the techniques themselves.

3. *Road Hustler* by Robert C. Prus and C.R.D. Sharper, 1977, expanded edition published by Kaufman and Greenberg. Hard to find but invaluable to the serious student, this is a close analysis of a real (and anonymous) card cheat. Not only are techniques discussed, but this book delves into the psychology of establishing trust, and even deeper into the psyche of the cheat.

Acknowledgments

All of the following people have two things in common. All of them provided invaluable assistance on this project. And at one time or another, each of them picked a card (and I'm happy to report that in all cases, I found the right one). Thanks, everyone, for watching my tricks and helping make this book what it is.

Joshua Jay's Book of Amazing Card Tricks has been years in the making. I wrote the first draft in 2003 in France, where I had access to some of the finest card magicians in the world and the world's largest playing card museum. Thanks to Bebel and Sebastien Clergue for early inspiration, and to Le Musée Français de la Carte à Jouer for letting me stay late and touch stuff I wasn't supposed to. Thanks also to playing card experts Tom and Judy Dawson and Cláudio Décourt for answering a few important questions.

A very early draft of this book became my senior thesis; my gratitude to Michelle Herman, my thesis advisor (and favorite professor), and Cameron Filipour and Christopher Coake.

I am ever indebted to my brain trust and most cherished readers: Rod Doiron, Jason England, Trisha Ferruccio, Joel Givens, Andi Gladwin, Raj Madhok, and Tyler Wilson.

Special thanks to Max Maven for his expertise in so many areas, and for his friendship. And to Jason England, whose knowledge of gambling history is incredible.

Eric Anderson and I collaborated on the breathtaking ephemera photos throughout the book, and I thank him for his excellent work. We spent many long hours photographing fascinating and rare cheating equipment, and I offer thanks to Doug Edwards and Simon Lovell, who generously made their valuable, fragile collections available to us. Thanks also to "Mr. M.," another friend who loaned me two rare pieces that appear in these pages—as promised, he shall remain anonymous.

This book wouldn't be in your hands if not for the enthusiastic support of James Levine, Suzie Bolotin, and Peter Workman. Many thanks to Megan Nicolay, my editor and friend, who is becoming scary-good with a pack of cards. And to the rest of the team at Workman: Anne Kerman, Janet Vicario, Julie Duquet, Tom Boyce,

Kristin Matthews, Selina Meere, and many others. And for support with the photo shoot: Kristin Folk, Cristina Pandrea, Christine Choe, Nate Lifton, and Liz Davis.

To my management team, James Diener, Randy Jackson, and Charlie Walk: You have all my gratitude for believing in me and helping me achieve my dreams.

Thanks to my family, who have endured more card tricks than anyone alive: The Martuccios, the Cohens, Rocco Ferruccio, David Jay, and Patricia Michaels. And to my mom, for her unbounded support for everything important to me.

Credits

CHAPTER 1
ALL HANDS ON DECK

The topics of this chapter—spreads, fans, flourishes—are always popular with card handlers. The originators of these techniques are unknown except where otherwise noted. The One-Handed Fan technique was taught to me personally by magician Bob Rees. His method is otherwise unpublished.

Ricky Jay, one-time world record–holder and accomplished sleight-of-hand artist, authored the definitive book on throwing cards, *Cards as Weapons,* 1977, Darien Books.

My other sources included:

Card Manipulations and *More Card Manipulations* by Jean Hugard, 1934–36, republished by Dover.

Expert Card Technique by Jean Hugard and Frederick Braue, 1940, republished by Dover.

"Slithering Snakes and Slick Spreads": *National Geographic* article by Jeremy Berlin, March 2010, page 26.

"Where do playing cards come from?": Playing cards were (and often still are) different from region to region. Suits are sometimes made up of coins, batons, swords, cups, acorns, bells, or leaves. And even the amount of cards in packs vary: In Italy and Spain, many decks consist of only 32 cards.

See W. Benham Gurney, *Playing Cards: The History and Secrets of the Pack,* Spring Books, London, date unknown, p. 1.

"Where did the expression 'not playing with a full deck' come from?": In 1628 the English government established the Worshipful Company of Makers of

Playing Cards to combat the foreign brands that dominated the marketplace. The company still exists today and is the premiere British manufacturer of cards. One of my favorite provisions from their constitution: No person using the trade may teach the trade or reveal "any of the secrets, skill, or misterys of the said Art or Trade" to anyone not a freeman of the company. The idea, of course, was to keep the manufacture of playing cards for British people within the borders of Britain.

See W. Benham Gurney, *Playing Cards: The History and Secrets of the Pack,* Spring Books, London, date unknown, p. 60.

CHAPTER 2
TRICKS

The Card Shark: The general concept of this effect was invented by V. F. Grant in 1932.

One Ahead: This classic card effect was first printed by Horatio Galasso in 1593. And it remains one of the most effective principles in card magic. I came across this effect in *Gibecière,* Vol. 2, No. 2, which is a complete translation of Galasso's original *Giochi di Carte Bellissimi.*

Barely Lift a Finger: This is "Impromptu Haunted Deck" by Bert Fenn. See *Pallbearer's Review,* January 1974, p. 704. It is based on a principle in Charles Jordan's "The Deck That Cuts Itself" from *Thirty Card Mysteries* (1919).

Friction Four: Retaining the top and bottom cards in each hand while throwing goes back to master card expert Johann Hofzinser's "The Four Eights" in *Kartenkünste* (1910, English translation 1931), written by Ottokar Fischer and translated into English by S. H. Sharpe.

"How are playing cards made?": See Leo Behnke, *The Making of Playing Cards,* Lybrary.com edition, 2005, p. 9.

"Can cards tell time?": The anomaly about sum of the letters in the names of the thirteen values equaling 52 described in the third bullet point is included here courtesy of Max Maven.

CHAPTER 3
SHUFFLE BORED

The chapter title is a play on words coined by my esteemed friend and fellow magician Simon Aronson, who used the title for an inspiring card trick and booklet in 1980, and then collected it in *Bound to Please*, 1994.

Hindu Shuffle: The Hindu appellation comes from Jean Hugard who introduced it in the first volume of his *Card Manipulations* in 1934, but the shuffle itself predates this.

Tabled Riffle Shuffle: Martin Nash passed away in 2009, and he was most supportive of this project. He was kind to me in my formative years, and it was with great sadness that I changed the passage about him from present to past tense.

Overhand Shuffle: This shuffle goes back at least as far as 1584. We know this because Reginald Scot describes how to cheat using this shuffle in his *Discoverie of Witchcraft*, arguably the first book containing card tricks in the English language.

Faro Shuffle: The first execution of a one-handed Faro Shuffle was likely by Howard de Courcy, in the early 1940s. Colleague Tyler Wilson has this to say about the origins of the faro shuffle: "The idea of perfectly interweaving cards during a shuffle—such as in a faro shuffle—was published in *The Whole Art and Mystery of Modern Gaming Fully Expos'd and Detected; Containing An Historical Account Of all the Secret Abuses Practis'd in the Game of Chance* (1726), written by an anonymous author who refers to himself only as 'Your Lordship's Most obliged and most obedient humble Servant.'"

Double Bridge: This technique is credited to Andreas Edmüller (*Card College*, Vol. 4, p. 1017). Steve Beam was the first to publish a controlled separation after the bridge.

False Cut: Jay Ose popularized this clever, counterintuitive ruse. See Harry Lorayne, *Close-Up Card Magic*, 1962, p. 93. Its progenitor is Richard Himber's False Cut, published in *The Tarbell System* in 1926. Magician and historian Roberto Giobbi has managed to track the cut back to 1896: Conradi-Horster published "Falsches Mischen" in his book, *Der Moderne Kartenkünstler*.

"Shuffling cards is cool. But what is *un*-shuffling?": The world record for card sorting is organized annually by the German Association of Mind Training. See recordholders.org/en/records/cardsorting.html

Information on the prison card-sorting program can be found on the Warm Springs Correctional Center: doc.nv.gov/?q=node/31

David Pepka pointed out this prison program to me; he insists his knowledge of it is not from experience.

CHAPTER 4
CHEAP TRICKS & SAFE BETS

Shiners: The use of shiners by gambling cheats dates back at least as far as 1530. They're also called "light."

Memorizing a Deck: The key card was first published in 1593 in the aforementioned *Giochi di Carte Bellissimi*, by Horatio Galasso.

Flipped: The standard title for this classic stunt is "The Circus Card Trick." The originator is unknown, but in references starting around 1940, it is always described as being very old. For more, see Fred Braue and Jean Hugard, *The Royal Road to Card Magic*, 1949, p. 138.

FOREWORD

David Blaine is a magician who has elevated the art of magic and is best known for living in very strange places (block of ice, water tank, small boxes).

LAST WORDS

"Take Care and Take Cards." Thanks to magician Steve Beam for permission to use this phrase, with which he closed every issue of *The Trapdoor* during his 15-year tenure as editor.

Behold, four Kings in majesty rever'd,
With hoary whiskers and a forky beard;
And four fair Queens whose hands sustain a flow'r,
Four Knaves in garbs succinct, a trust band,
Caps on their heads, and halberds in their hand;
And particolour'd troops, a shining train,
Draw forth to combat on the velvet plain.

With his broad sabre next, a chief in years,
The hoary Majesty of Spades appears,
Puts forth one manly leg, to sight reveal'd,
The rest, his many-colour'd robe conceal'd.
The rebel Knave, who dares his prince engage,
Proves the just victim of his royal rage.
Ev'n mighty Pam [*Knave of Clubs*], that Kings and Queens o'erthrew
And mow'd down armies in the fights of Lu,
Sad chance of war! now destitute of aid,
Falls undistinguish'd by the victor spade!

—ALEXANDER POPE, *The Rape of the Lock*, 1712